Picture-Perfect

Worry-Free
Weddings

72 DESTINATIONS AND VENUES

Diane Warner

Due to the constantly changing nature of the wedding, honeymoon and travel industries, including prices quoted for their services, neither the author nor the publisher makes any guarantees as to availability, quality, costs or features described, nor does either warranty products or services rendered by any vendor or organization mentioned in this book. Likewise, mention of any product, service, vendor or organization does not signify endorsement or recommendation by the author or publisher.

Other fine Betterway Books are available from your local bookstore or direct from the publisher.

02 01 00 99 98   5 4 3 2 1

Library of Congress Cataloging-in-Publication Data

Warner, Diane.
   Picture-perfect worry-free weddings : 72 destinations and venues / Diane Warner.—1st ed.
     p.   cm.
  Includes index.
  ISBN 1-55870-479-5 (alk. paper)
   1. Weddings—Planning. 2. Hotels—Guidebooks. 3. Resorts—Guidebooks. 4. Travel—Guidebooks. 5. Honeymoons. I. Title.
HQ745.W38 1998
395.2'2—dc21   97-50086
                                                      CIP

Edited by David Borcherding
Production edited by Saundra Hesse
Interior designed by Jannelle Schoonover
Cover designed by Angela Lennert Wilcox
Cover photography by Comstock

ACKNOWLEDGMENTS

First of all, I would like to thank my editor, David Borcherding. I would also like to thank my research assistant, Linda Glass, and all the couples who so graciously agreed to share their stories in this book. Finally, many thanks to Gerard J. Monaghan, President of the Association of Bridal Consultants, and the seven Master Bridal Consultants who shared their advice and case histories for the benefit of my readers. Thanks to all of you for helping make this book a success!

To Beth Bryan, my wonderful friend for over 35 years

Table of Contents

INTRODUCTION 1

CHAPTER 1 3
The Venue Wedding

CHAPTER 2 21
The Destination Wedding Inside Mainland U.S.

CHAPTER 3 42
The Destination Wedding Outside Mainland U.S.

CHAPTER 4 68
The Informal Wedding

CHAPTER 5 85
The Do-It-Yourself Worry-Free Wedding

CHAPTER 6 113
The Professionally Planned Wedding

EPILOGUE 143

APPENDIX 144

INDEX 153

I have wonderful news for you! It *is* possible to have a worry-free wedding with very little pre-marital stress! If you don't know what I'm talking about, just wander into any bridal showroom some Saturday morning and survey the scene as the brides paw frantically through the racks of wedding gowns; or eavesdrop on the bride and her mother as a florist presents his seven basic wedding packages; or even better yet, spend a couple days perusing the postings on any of the World Wide Web's wedding newsgroups. You'll find out why "stress" and "hassle" are the latest buzz words in the wedding industry today.

Gone are the days of "Wedding Sticker Shock" that catapulted the bride's parents into clinical depression when they discovered how much their daughter's wedding would cost. Today's families are well aware of the average $20,000 price tag; they don't like it, but it no longer shocks them.

The new "shocker" is the enormous amount of stress generated by planning a wedding. This is due partly to the fact that the wedding industry has grown by cosmic leaps in this country, generating hundreds of new options that "really must be included" and trendy new things that "really should be done," all of which have expanded and complicated the planning process. Add to that the fact that the average length of a couple's engagement has increased to fifteen months, which serves to multiply the angst even further, leaving the bride and groom stressed to the max by the time the big day finally arrives.

Stress has become such a mammoth problem, in fact, that a new phenomenon has evolved: psychologists and professional stress counselors who specialize in helping couples cope with the anxieties of planning their weddings. Myrna Ruskin, a Certified Stress Management Counselor in New York City, now devotes her entire practice to counseling and encouraging couples through her seminars, one-on-one counseling sessions and a thirty-minute cassette tape she has created entitled, "How to Get Married Without Feeling Harried." I've listened to her tape, and she's right on with her advice, but isn't it amazing that it has come to this: The need for private counselors and instructional tapes to help us survive the complexities and anxieties of planning a wedding?

It's no wonder so many brides and grooms are asking the question: "Isn't there a better way to get married without so many hassles?" There are several ways, and that's what this book is all about. Whether your wedding budget is $1,000 or $50,000; whether you want a wedding that's formal or informal; and whether this is your first marriage or not, there *can* be a worry-free wedding in your future. The choice depends on your own personal tastes and circumstances.

If you have an especially sticky family situation, for instance, with several difficult relationship problems that must be resolved before you can plan your wedding; or if you've been married before and already "been there, done that," you may prefer a Destination Wedding. Or, if you're really short on time, patience or money, a Surprise Wedding or a Combination Wedding may be the answer. Of course, if you really want that big, traditional dream wedding after all, I have three more ideas for you to consider.

As you read along, weighing these worry-free wedding options, you'll also be encouraged by the Success Stories sprinkled throughout the book. These are stories of actual brides and grooms whose weddings were worry-free. I've found, after leading hundreds of wedding seminars and talking to engaged couples all over the country, what helps you the most is to "show" rather than "tell." You thrive on true stories—case histories of real, live brides and grooms whose worry-free weddings prove it can be done.

Interviewing these couples, by the way, was the greatest joy of writing this book. I heard some of the most touching, poignant, interesting love stories of men and women who met, fell in love and were married. What fascinated me most was the diversity of their ages, careers, family backgrounds and wedding styles. I know you'll enjoy their stories as much as I did.

Happy reading, and as you plan your wedding day, my heart goes out to you. You want to eliminate the stress and anxiety of planning your wedding, and that's exactly what I want for you too!

CHAPTER ONE

The Venue Wedding

The Venue Wedding—sometimes called a One-Stop Wedding—provides an all-in-one wedding package with a site coordinator who makes all the arrangements for your ceremony and reception at one location in or near your hometown. The packages usually include everything in one price—decorations, flowers, music, photography, videography, reception food, wedding cake and, in many cases, the officiant as well. It's a simple, practical concept.

Advantages

- Wonderful for the bride and groom whose demanding careers don't allow the time or energy necessary to plan a wedding from scratch.
- The bride and groom can relax and enjoy their engagement period.

Disadvantages

- Relinquishes hands-on control of most of the wedding plans. (For the bride and groom who have the time and prefer to build their wedding day from scratch, see Chapter Five, "The Do-It-Yourself Worry-Free Wedding.")

If you like the idea of a Venue Wedding, you may wonder where you can find this kind of one-stop shopping. Some hotel chains and resorts offer all-in-one wedding packages, as do a few inns, bed and breakfasts, lodges, castles, mansions, country estates, cruise and yacht companies, private clubs, wineries, restaurants and various nature or wilderness venues. Most, of course, offer to cater wedding receptions on their sites, but what you want is a venue that plans *everything*—including the ceremony itself.

It takes a bit of calling around to find one of these all-inclusive venues within a reasonable distance of your home. The concept is catching on fast, however, so you may be surprised at the number you'll find that offer these package deals.

The best way to acquaint you with the worry-free advantages of one of these Venue Weddings is to tell you about various sites I've discovered as I've traveled around the country. The services offered by these venues are typical of what you might expect to find near your hometown. By the way, the sample venues I've included here, along with others featured in the book, are referenced in the appendix, just in case a specific venue sounds like a possibility for your own wedding. Also, note that any prices stated here were current as this book went to press and are subject to change.

A Garden Wedding

A garden makes a lovely setting for a wedding, but the trick is to find one that is part of a facility that offers all-inclusive wedding services. Many inns, historical mansions and country estates fall into this category. Troutbeck and East Fork Country Estate are two examples.

TROUTBECK

Troutbeck is an old English country estate nestled among 442 gentle acres in Amenia, New York, a two-hour drive from New York City. Troutbeck is known for its Country Inn Wedding Weekends where you can be married in one of many photogenic settings, backdropped by two-hundred-foot-high sycamores, a babbling brook and sumptuous gardens.

Troutbeck also offers a full-scale cocktail dinner-dance that lasts for five hours, including the ceremony, or a less elaborate three-hour cocktail party reception. The food is rated four star, so you're guaranteed to be pleased with the cuisine and exquisite presentation.

A typical wedding package includes use of the facility for five hours, open bar, hors d'oeuvres, wedding meal and cake, and the services of a wedding specialist who will coordinate all the wedding plans, at prices that range from about $100 to $150 per person. This is in addition to the costs of the flowers, photography and music. Guest rooms are also available at a reduced rate.

Troutbeck is a wonderful example of a garden wedding venue.

EAST FORK COUNTRY ESTATE

East Fork Country Estate is situated on a knoll with a spectacular view of Mount Hood, just south of Gresham, Oregon. The flowering gardens that surround the estate house embellish the warm, relaxed country setting. East Fork was designed specifically for elegant weddings and receptions.

The ceremony takes place in a quaint country gazebo with up to 225 guests seated under white canopies on lawn areas. The reception is held in a large room in the estate house with bay windows facing Mount Hood to the east and overlooking a lush valley to the south. There are also three covered patio areas and white canopies that cover several lawns.

East Fork offers full-service packages for 50 to 225 guests. Packages include the services of a wedding consultant to help plan the wedding and reception and a wedding coordinator who attends the wedding rehearsal and coordinates all the ceremony and reception arrangements.

East Fork Country Estate is another fine example of a garden wedding venue.

A Bed and Breakfast Wedding

Bed and breakfasts are becoming increasingly popular as venue wedding sites, especially those that offer the kind of all-inclusive services necessary for a worry-free wedding. For some reason most couples don't think of a B&B as a wedding venue, but it is actually a wonderfully quirky, delightfully different site to consider. Most bed and breakfasts are in historical buildings where real people have slept, made love, sung and laughed over decades of time. Here are two examples that will whet your interest in these alternatives.

CAPTAIN WALSH HOUSE

Captain Walsh House in Benicia, California, is one of the most popular wedding venues in the Bay Area. Located in Benicia's signature historic district, it is a historically significant 150-year-old inn with unique, gracious Gothic charm. The house was originally commissioned to be built for Gen. M.G. Vallejo's daughter, Epiphania, as a gift for her marriage to Lt. John Frisbie. It was designed by prominent architect Andrew Jackson Downing, built in Boston, then dismantled and shipped 'round the Horn. It was re-erected in Benicia in 1849 for the newlywed couple and eventually acquired by Eleanor and Captain Walsh.

Captain Walsh House was featured on the cover of a recent *Better Homes and Gardens Bedroom & Bath* as one of the three best decorated inns in the United States. The weddings take place in the romantic West Garden in front of a wedding arch, followed by receptions that have to be seen to be believed, with elegant detail given to the banquet table, cake table and bar service. The entire inn, in fact, is "done up royal" for each wedding, incorporating yards and yards of fabric and hundreds of fresh flowers.

The inn's facility rates range from $1,000 to $1,750 and everything else is extra, from catering ($22 to $30 per person) to beverage service ($3 per hour per guest) to rentals, florals, minister, music, cake, photographer, tent rental and wait staff.

An assortment of musicians is available, from string quartets to jazz ensemble to the staff harpist who performs on a concert gold harp. Chefs at the inn are San Francisco Culinary Academy trained and are renowned for their elegant presentation.

I was furnished with references to many happy couples who were married at Captain Walsh House, all of whom raved over the staff's professionalism and their attention to detail. Here are some of the couples' kudos:

"You both have been wonderful in the planning of our wedding. It was perfect. Our 'fairy-tale wedding' came true."

"We appreciate your taking care of the details and making sure everything went smoothly. We enjoyed it so much, we'd like to celebrate it all again."

"The wedding was one of the best days of our lives. It was warm, beautiful and full of love."

Meanwhile, if you're thinking of booking Captain Walsh House, you'll need to do it way in advance because it stays fully booked months ahead of time, especially during the summer wedding season.

SARA'S BED AND BREAKFAST INN

Sara's is located in the historic Houston Heights section of Houston, Texas, in a neighborhood long recognized for its diversity of turn-of-the-century architectural styles. It was originally built as a Victorian cottage and changed hands many times over the years, although some of its earliest owners were Claude Taylor, and later, John Franklow, both railroad men.

The charming courtyard and glass-enclosed Garden Room have become popular settings for weddings, and family and members of the wedding party usually reserve all fourteen rooms in the inn for a wedding weekend.

Sara's Queen Anne Wedding Package includes:

- Use of the entire lower portion common area of the inn, which includes the 1,000-square-foot Garden Room, plus the 600-square-foot covered Garden Arbor
- One-hour rehearsal the evening before the wedding
- Choice of ceremony areas, which include the Front Porch, Front Stairway, Garden Room and Covered Garden Arbor
- Dressing room for the bride
- Choice of taped bridal music
- Church-style seating with white wood chairs for up to one hundred guests
- Decorations, including hurricane lanterns with candle centerpieces surrounded by mixed silk flower wreaths, plus decorated stairway
- Reception food, including elegant croissant sandwiches, fruit trays, quiche, vegetable tray, spinach dip, cheese ball, wedding cake, punch and coffee
- Cake knife, server, toasting goblets, feather pen for guest book, food servers, setup and cleanup

All of this for a twenty-five-guest minimum of $1,600, plus $18 per additional person. Optional extras include a groom's cake, starting at $60, plus the bridal suite for $110 per night or a flat fee for reservation of the entire inn.

What an easy, affordable idea this is for a small wedding.

If you like the idea of being married at a full-service bed and breakfast, look for a romantic, reputable site in your area. For a listing of bed and breakfasts, pick up one of the books listed in the appendix or contact the American Bed and Breakfast Association.

A Nature Wedding

There are countless natural, outdoor wedding sites around the country, and it's just a matter of finding a company who specializes in making arrangements for a favorite site within a reasonable distance of your hometown.

SEDONA, ARIZONA

Weddings in Sedona is an example of one of these companies. Sandy Ezrine, its owner, has planned over two hundred weddings in and around Sedona, Arizona, which is considered to be one of the most beautiful places on earth. Although she arranges weddings for a great variety of sites—including a chapel, a resort and a Flight of Love wedding on a mesa with delivery by helicopter— the company specializes in nature weddings. Some of these outdoor ceremonies take place in an intimate redwood gazebo, on a ranch, beside the romantic Love Tree, among Sedona's beautiful red rocks or at the foot of Two Lovers Butte beside the rapids of Oak Creek.

Sandy told me her weddings range from large and elaborate to simple and sweet, such as one that included only the couple and their cocker spaniel and another where the bride and groom recited their vows on horseback. (One local wedding she thankfully *wasn't* asked to plan was a "biker wedding" where the bride and groom arrived on their motorcycles stark naked!)

Her services are all-inclusive, including the flowers, photography, music, videography, decorations, reception food, wedding cake, hair stylist, manicurist, makeup artist, limousine service, helicopter service and, of course, arrangements for the ceremony and reception sites, including a customized ceremony with a minister and witnesses, if requested. She also arranges lodging for the bridal couple and wedding guests in the Sedona area.

Sandy's company coordinates everything and absorbs all the wedding stress, as evidenced by my interview with Mimi and Brian, a couple whose wedding took place at Red Rock Crossing above Sedona. Here is their story.

Mimi and Brian Kelly

Mimi and Brian Kelly met on a blind date that was arranged by two blind ladies. This takes some explanation.

Mimi and Brian were both well established in their careers—he in the semiconductor business and she in the sale of consulting services. Both had been divorced for several years and each had recently purchased a new home in Chandler, Arizona—in subdivisions on opposite sides of town. Because each owned a brand-new home, they needed to purchase blinds for their windows. The day Brian's window coverings were installed he asked the two women who owned the blind company if they ever met any nice single ladies when they were out bidding on jobs around town. They said they did and that they would keep their eyes peeled.

Mimi happened to order blinds from these same two women, and when they came to her home they asked her, "How would you like to meet a really nice guy?"

She said, "Listen, I've dated every loser in the state of Arizona. I'm not interested."

They said, "But he's really cute—he looks just like Mel Gibson."

Mimi replied, "Mel Gibson, huh? Well, maybe."

And so the two blind women set Mimi and Brian up on a blind date. Mimi liked him right away—he was really nice, a lot of fun and had a great sense of humor. The feeling wasn't mutual, however, at least not at first. Brian's reaction was that he didn't want to be her "boyfriend"—"ever," only her "friend." Mimi said, "Fine, that's all right with me."

Not too long after they met, Brian's job took him to Italy for three months and during that time he and Mimi got to know each other better via e-mail. The friendship finally began to turn to something a little deeper—at least in Mimi's mind—when she went to Italy to visit him. Before Brian left for Italy he had told her, "No one would come all the way over to Italy to visit me while I'm there."

She said, "I would."

He said, "You *would*?" And she did.

Mimi felt that their relationship changed while they were in Italy together, but she wasn't sure how Brian felt until they returned to Arizona and he called his family about coming over for Thanksgiving dinner. He said, "I'd like to bring my girlfriend."

Ah, "girlfriend"—progress!

In the months that followed they became even closer until one day Brian asked Mimi, "Don't you think it's time we got married?"

Two years passed from the time they met until their outdoor wedding on April 26, 1997, in Red Rock State Park in Sedona. Their wedding was planned for them by Sandy Ezrine of Weddings in Sedona who made all the arrangements, including the photographer, videographer, the flowers and the music—a flautist playing a silver flute for the ceremony and a guitarist who played classic rock and roll during the reception. She also arranged for the ceremony and reception sites at Red Rock Crossing, plus the reception food, all the decorations and the officiant—her husband.

Sandy even helped Mimi find a wedding dress at a store called The Victorian Cowgirl in Sedona. Mimi wanted a simple dress she could wear again and found just the thing: a long, gauzy, ivory sleeveless sundress. She felt it was perfect for the natural streamside ceremony setting.

The couple's seventy guests were told to dress "casual" with comfortable walking shoes because they would need to walk down a long path to the creek where the ceremony would take place. Because of its natural ambience, the ceremony site needed very little in the way of decorations—only an arch entwined with wildflowers. The reception site, the Crescent Moon Pavilion, is a covered picnic area where the catered wedding lunch was served: barbecued chicken, steak, roasted potatoes and tossed salad. The tables were covered with purple and ivory tablecloths with wildflowers in clay pots.

Mimi and Brian's Sedona wedding had seventy guests and cost

less than $4,500, including the catered lunch. The wedding day was exactly what they had dreamed it would be, and when I asked Mimi about the stress factor, she said, "This has been the most stress-free thing I've ever done. Sandy took care of everything. Everything went off without a hitch, and no one ever had any reason to be nervous."

Definitely a "success story," don't you agree? ♡

A Hotel or Resort Wedding

Although hotels and resorts have always been happy to host a wedding reception, only recently have some begun to offer all-inclusive services for both the ceremony and reception. Some independent hotels and resorts offer these services, as well as certain hotel chains, ranging from Hyatt Regency resorts, which offer upper-scale packages, to Holiday Inn, which offers more economical packages.

HYATT REGENCY RESORTS

Most Hyatt Regency resorts offer complete wedding packages, plus honeymoon accommodations, too, if you'd like, and each provides a wedding specialist or special events coordinator who will make all the arrangements.

To give you an idea of the services offered, let me tell you about the Hyatt Regency Monterey in Monterey, California, which provides a special events coordinator to handle all of your wedding day plans. Here is a list of some of the services provided:

- Complete wedding day planning
- Reception planning
- Food selection and presentation
- Wedding cake
- Formal-wear rentals
- Flowers
- Photography
- Videography
- Music

- Entertainment
- Limousine service
- Officiant

In addition, the coordinator will help you determine your budget, arrange pre-wedding meetings with the officiant, select your wedding music, choose your flowers and decorations, plan accommodations for your out-of-town guests, arrange your rehearsal dinner, coordinate your transportation, arrange your bridesmaids' luncheon, select a theme for your reception, and so forth.

One thing I love about this particular Hyatt is the choice of clever, creative theme dinners, including British Invasion, Bier Garten, South of the Border Buffet, Crosby Style Clambake, Western Barbecue, and Italian Trattoria.

To top it off, the Hyatt Regency Monterey presents the bride and groom with a wedding gift that consists of a complimentary wedding night stay and a bottle of champagne.

This particular Hyatt Regency has several lovely ceremony sites to choose from, including an impressive gazebo that borders the golf course, but they can also arrange for an off-premise site, if you would prefer. Of course, the Carmel-Monterey area is loaded with romantic, photogenic settings.

By the way, although I have listed the Hyatt worldwide reservations phone number in the appendix, I discovered that none of their central reservations clerks seems to be aware of the specific wedding or honeymoon packages available at the various Hyatt Regency locations, whether inside or outside of the United States. Their expertise seems to be limited to making room reservations, although they are more than happy to furnish you with the telephone number of any of their Hyatts, which you should call direct to inquire about specific wedding and honeymoon packages.

Of course, if you're planning a venue wedding within a reasonable distance of your home, you should be able to locate the closest Hyatt Regency through your local telephone directory.

HOLIDAY INN

Don't turn your nose up at the idea of having your ceremony and reception at a Holiday Inn; you'll be surprised to see what a terrific job they do for the money!

As you may know, most Holiday Inns feature an enormous swimming pool in a tropical setting, a perfect venue for a wedding with a Polynesian theme. You can float flowers or candles on the water, or a raft with musicians playing Hawaiian music.

Here is an example of a wedding package offered by the Holiday Inn in Willowbrook, Illinois. For a total of $22.95 per person, plus tax and tip, they provide all of this:

- Wedding reception with skirted tables, choice of four-course dinner, plus dessert
- One-hour cocktail reception before dinner
- Three-hour open bar after dinner
- Champagne or wine toast for all guests
- Wedding cake in the style, color and decoration of your choice
- Fresh flower in bud vase on each table
- Coffee service during cake cutting
- Attended coat check service
- Complimentary guest room for the bride and groom on their wedding night
- Up to three complimentary rooms for the immediate family
- Breakfast for the bride and groom the following morning
- Three hours of complimentary limousine service for all weddings of two hundred or more guests
- Limousine transportation to Midway or O'Hare airport for the bride and groom

Of course, you'll need to furnish your own officiant for the ceremony itself, but you can't beat their all-inclusive price for everything else.

THE SAGAMORE

In addition to hotel chains, many independent resort hotels offer all-inclusive wedding services. An excellent example is The Sagamore on Lake George at Bolton Landing, New York.

The Sagamore's specialist coordinates all your wedding plans, including the rehearsal dinner, the reception, floral packages, wedding cake, limousine and guest transportation, music (they have an excellent selection of DJs and bands to choose from), entertainment, photographer, justice of the peace and, of course, overnight accommodations.

The quality of the reception food and its presentation must be seen to be believed. The Sagamore Brunch features their renowned ice carving, plus such specialties as Smoked Fish Mirror, Cassoulet of Chicken and Garlic Sausage, Sea Bass, Rock Shrimp and Bay Scallop Ragout and, in addition to the wedding cake, truffles, bonbons and chocolate-dipped strawberries.

The Sagamore also offers an exquisite, formal wedding dinner package that includes white-glove service and is preceded by an elegant one-hour reception of butlered hors d'oeuvres.

QUAIL LODGE RESORT

Quail Lodge Resort and Golf Club is the only five-star resort located between San Francisco and Los Angeles. It is nestled among 850 beautifully landscaped acres that boast miles of jogging and hiking trails, an eighteen-hole championship golf course, arched footbridges, lighted fountains and ten sparkling lakes with swans and other wildlife. An experienced full-time wedding coordinator takes care of absolutely *all* the arrangements, beginning with your choice of scenic outdoor or indoor setting, such as the picturesque arched bridge at Mallard Lake or the lush lawns at Quail Meadows Lake, under a stylish canopy, in a festive tent or in one of their many elegant party rooms.

My favorite site is Quail Meadows Lake, one of the most romantic wedding settings I've ever seen. As the guests watch in awe from the flower-bedecked ceremony site on the shores of the lake, the father of the bride slowly escorts his beautiful daughter in an elegant white horse-drawn carriage. They start from afar and as the carriage draws closer and closer, you can't help but thrill to the glory of it—it takes "Here Comes the Bride" to a whole new dimension!

I don't need to list the all-inclusive services provided by the resort's wedding coordinator because your wish is her desire, and everything she plans will be taken care of without a single glitch. This is a superb example of the quintessential "worry-free one-stop wedding shop."

FOUR SEASONS HOTEL

The Four Seasons Hotel in Chicago is considered to be one of the top hotels in the nation, noted for its elegant decor, award-winning cuisine and gracious service. And when it comes to service, their all-inclusive wedding planning services are beyond compare. Not only do they work with a professional consultant who arranges for your choice of floral packages, disc jockey or orchestra, photographer, videographer, calligrapher, makeup artist, hair stylist, transportation and ministerial services, but they also arrange for these extras as well:

- Customized reception meal
- Table placecards and printed menus especially designed for the reception meal
- Complimentary suite for the bride and groom on the wedding night
- Complimentary changing rooms for the bridesmaids and groomsmen
- Setup and coordination of sleeping rooms for the bridal party and guests
- Gourmet gift baskets and favors to be delivered to the rooms of the bridal party and guests
- Airline reservations and confirmations
- A bonded babysitter for attending families
- Coordination of limousine transportation and/or a horse-drawn carriage ride

The luxurious hotel, with its grand staircase and other elegant settings, ensures memorable photographs for the couple's album.

The Four Seasons does it all, just as you would expect from a world-renowned five-diamond hotel. In fact, their motto is "Above and Beyond," assuring a totally worry-free wedding in all respects.

An On-the-Water Wedding

Water always seems to create a romantic ambience for a wedding, which is probably why so many couples get married aboard yachts, ferryboats, paddleboats and stationary cruise ships.

I'd like to tell you about one of these in particular—the Queen Mary in Long Beach, California, whose all-inclusive services are typical of this type of wedding venue.

THE QUEEN MARY

The Queen Mary is an ocean liner that is permanently berthed in Long Beach Harbor. This elegant ship is an ideal wedding venue that offers the services of an experienced wedding coordinator who plans everything for the couple, including the rehearsal dinner, the wedding ceremony and the reception.

Wedding packages ranging from $2,000 to $2,500 include, in addition to the services of a personal wedding coordinator, the use of the Royal Wedding Chapel; chapel flowers; ceremony rehearsal; changing room for the bride; personalized invitations and thank-you cards; flowers for the bride, groom, maid of honor and best man; guest book and pen; the bride's garter; crystal wedding cake top; cake knife and server; toasting goblets; musical selections; full photography service; and overnight accommodations for the newlyweds. Also available are the services of the ship's captain or another officiant to perform the wedding ceremony.

In addition, the coordinator will arrange elegant wedding receptions for ten to two thousand guests, including hors d'oeuvres, champagne, sparkling cider, a full luncheon or dinner menu and the couple's choice of wedding cake, starting at about $29 per person for lunch and about $34 for dinner. The reception may be held in one of sixteen richly decorated salons, on deck with the cool ocean breezes and skyline views, or in the engine room among the exhibits, pipes and boilers, for those who prefer a truly unique setting for their special day.

The Queen Mary also offers three harbor-view restaurants for pre-wedding breakfasts, bridal luncheons, "get to know the family" dinners or rehearsal dinners.

This grand old lady of the seas is indeed a special site for a wedding and reception but, more importantly, it offers easy, worry-free wedding packages for today's couples, one of whom is Lee and Ingeborg (Inge) Dickerson who were married aboard the Queen Mary on January 2, 1997. I had the privilege of interviewing them, and here is their story.

Lee and Inge Dickerson

Lee Dickerson, age 74, and Inge Kremeyer, age 67, fell in love in 1949. They met at an American military base in northwestern Germany when he was a serviceman involved in the effort to get supplies into the blockaded city of Berlin. She was a German clerk in the paymaster's office. They dated for many months, enjoying long walks in the woods and Germany's beautiful parks, until he was called back to the United States. Although he was denied reassignment to Germany, his love letters scorched the mailbags that traversed the distance between them.

Eventually, however, they lost contact with one another. Each married someone else and Inge moved to the United States where she became a citizen. They both became widowed, she in 1973 and he in 1993, and although they never tried to contact each other, she saved his love letters for all those years. She recalled, "Every now and then I would read them and cry." In fact, in January 1996, she pulled them out and read them over again, beginning with the last one he had written that said, "It isn't meant to be, Darling. I wish you a good life and God bless you."

This time, as she read his letters, a voice seemed to speak to her, and for days she thought about their long-lost relationship. Then she remembered one of her students who had retired from the United States Navy. She spoke with him, and he provided her with a telephone number for the Naval Retirement Center in St. Louis where she requested help in locating Lee.

She filled out the application and wrote a letter that was forwarded to Lee. He said, "I had wondered where she was, what she was doing, how she was getting along. I never knew she was in the United States. I never had any idea I would see her again."

As a result of her letter, Lee called Inge and they agreed to meet in Tucson, Arizona, where each had a son. When they met, Inge said,

"It was like no time had passed at all—forty-seven years were wiped away. My son was trying to act as chaperone, but I sent him away."

Following their reunion in Tucson, there were visits to her home in Chicago and his home in Torrance, California, where he had retired from the U. S. Air Force as a major in 1963 and from Hughes Aircraft as a contracts manager in 1985.

I asked Lee how long it took from the time of their reunion in Tucson until they knew they wanted to marry. He said there was never any doubt, that he knew from the moment he received her letter. So, I asked, "But did you formally propose to her? Down on one knee, and all?"

He laughed and said, "Oh, yes, I proposed formally—down on one knee as I gave her her engagement ring."

Well, their wedding and reception aboard the Queen Mary was something else! They were surrounded by seventy-five friends and relatives who traveled to Long Beach from as far away as Paris and Germany. It was a touching scene as this couple recited their vows—finally—after forty-seven years, Inge glowing and lovely in her beautiful dress and Lee quite handsome in his dark blue air force uniform.

Inge's two sons, Karl, 30, and Kevin, 28, are thrilled for their mother. Kevin said, "She's gone through a transformation—this is clearly something she wanted. You can't help but be thankful."

I asked Lee, "Was this wedding as worry-free as you thought it would be?" He said that the staff at the Queen Mary took care of everything. The only stress, he said, was all the hoopla caused by the dozens of reporters who were there to photograph and tape their wedding. There was even a reporter from CNN!

It didn't let up after the reception either, because Lee and Inge left the Queen Mary for an appearance on *Good Morning, America*. Lee told me, "There was so much excitement, we didn't get to bed on our wedding night until five in the morning!"

Well, all I know is that I've never talked to a happier groom in my life! In fact, they enjoyed their first honeymoon so much (to Hong Kong and Singapore) that they decided to take another honeymoon right away—this one to Hawaii. They are really enjoying each other's company, especially all the traveling, and I was lucky to squeeze in an interview between their trips. They were leaving on yet *another* honeymoon a few days after I had the privilege of speaking with them.

Congratulations, Lee and Inge! ♡

A Castle Wedding

There are hundreds of castles sprinkled all over America, and they have become popular all-inclusive venue wedding sites, especially those that are unusually grand or have great historical significance. Belhurst Castle is just one example.

BELHURST CASTLE

Belhurst Castle is a turreted red Medina stone structure nestled among sweeping lawns on the cliff side of Seneca Lake in Geneva, New York. It was constructed over a four-year period beginning in 1885 at an initial cost of $475,000, a fortune in the late 1800s. It has quite a romantic past, with rumors of secret tunnels and hidden treasures buried in the walls. It is listed on the National Register of Historic Places.

Outdoor weddings take place in front of the turreted castle on manicured lawns that meld into the deep blue waters of a glacier-fed freshwater lake. The setting is a photographer's dream.

The wedding reception is held in the elegant ambience of the Garden Room inside the castle, complete with white lace, silver candelabra, frosted ice carvings and sparkling champagne.

Belhurst Castle, like so many castles around the country, provides a professional wedding specialist who will make all your wedding and reception arrangements, whether you have your heart set on a harpist to play during your ceremony, a stilt-walking comedian to liven things up during the reception or a vintage Rolls Royce to "carry you off into the sunset." The specialist takes care of everything!

Whether you envision a formal Cinderella Wedding, a Renaissance Wedding or a Victorian Wedding, what could be more perfect than a castle venue?

I think a Venue Wedding makes a lot of sense. Why should the bride and groom and their families spend fifteen months agonizing over complicated wedding and reception plans when one venue can handle everything for them?

If a Venue Wedding sounds like a good worry-free idea to you, do a little research until you find a site you like. It should take you no more than an eight-hour day to find a spot you and your fiancé really love. Then you can both settle back into your careers, relax and let the site coordinator iron out all the hassles while you enjoy your engagement parties.

THINGS TO REMEMBER:

○ Never sign on the dotted line until you have personally spoken with at least three couples who were married at the site. The venue wedding coordinator should be able to furnish you with references.

○ Shy away from any venue where the wedding coordinator was hired "last week." Search until you find one that has an experienced professional wedding specialist who has been with the facility a minimum of one year.

○ Try to relax and let the site's wedding specialist plan your wedding and reception. Although she will discuss plans with you and offer various options, try to relinquish the control. Otherwise, you'll be taking the "worries" back onto your own shoulders.

○ Visit several venues before making your choice—don't feel rushed to book your site. If possible, "eavesdrop" on a wedding that is taking place, and check out the DJ or band provided by the venue. They won't know it, but they will be "auditioning" for your own wedding!

CHAPTER TWO

The Destination Wedding Inside Mainland U.S.

The Destination Wedding, also referred to as a Travel Wedding or a Honeymoon Wedding, takes place at the honeymoon site. It can be arranged in one of two ways:

- By the wedding coordinator on staff at the honeymoon hotel or resort
- By an independent destination wedding planner (also known as a travel wedding consultant) who plans destination weddings in various cities and countries

Here are the advantages and disadvantages of having a Destination Wedding:

Advantages

- It's usually much less expensive than the average hometown wedding.
- The stress involved in planning this type of wedding barely registers on the "wedding stress meter."
- It's a great way to avoid sticky family problems caused by personality conflicts, divorces and cultural, ethnic or religious differences.
- It solves the problem of feeling obligated to invite everyone from the workplace, church or school.
- It's a wonderful choice for the couple who has been married before and already "been there, done that."
- You don't need to travel between your wedding site and honeymoon site. Once you're married, you're already there!

- It's 100 percent guaranteed to avoid being the boring "cookie-cutter" wedding.

Disadvantages

- You usually aren't able to view the site until you arrive for the wedding (although videotapes of the resort's wedding sites are almost always available).
- Not *all* the really important people in your life may be able to afford to travel to your wedding (although it is common for the parents or the couple's two best friends to come along as a little vacation trip).
- The bride will need to bring her gown with her *on board* the plane (unless she chooses to wear native wedding attire, which has become quite popular, especially in places like Hawaii and Fiji).
- The couple may regret not having a big wedding reception (although someone will undoubtedly host a reception for them after the honeymoon, or the couple themselves can host a little party for their closest friends and family members where they can view the ceremony via videotape).

Read over these pros and cons one more time and see if you don't agree with me that the advantages far outweigh the disadvantages. If you're looking for a worry-free wedding idea, you can't beat a Destination Wedding. It's no wonder it has become so popular.

There are hundreds of destination wedding sites around the world, and an all-inclusive list would fill a book in itself. I have listed my own personal favorites in this book. To qualify for my list the sites had to pass these four tests:

1. Offer all-inclusive packages that include the services of an experienced, well-qualified wedding coordinator
2. Have a romantic setting
3. Have an excellent reputation
4. Have uncomplicated marriage license requirements

I divided my list into two categories: "Inside Mainland United States," which are described in this chapter, and "Outside Mainland United States," which are found in the next chapter.

A Disney Wedding
DISNEY'S FAIRY TALE WEDDINGS

As many of you already know if you've been watching *Weddings of a Lifetime* on Lifetime TV, Disney's Fairy Tale wedding is truly a fantasy. It can take place in the glass-enclosed Wedding Pavilion that is set on an island in the Seven Seas Lagoon, a truly magical site for the ceremony, followed by a Cinderella Reception at the Grand Floridian, or the ceremony can take place at one of a number of other locations. The Wedding Pavilion evokes images of a Victorian summer house and offers a picturesque view of Cinderella Castle.

Located at the Walt Disney World Resort near Orlando, Florida, this setting is one of the most magical on earth, with over 27,000 acres of luxury and excitement at its doorstep. Enjoy three unbelievable theme parks, five magnificent PGA championship golf courses, lighted tennis courts, three water parks, dozens of white sand beaches and glistening swimming pools, exciting nighttime entertainment, lush nature paths, horseback riding and miles of open waterways that beckon you to sail, ski or fish to your heart's content.

All of these activities are available at fourteen luxurious world-class resort hotels where Disney cast members guarantee to pamper you and your entire wedding party in pure Disney style.

Tucked within the pavilion is Franck's, an elegantly designed salon recreated from the movie "Father of the Bride," where you can plan every detail of your glorious wedding ceremony and reception with the help of Disney's Fairy Tale Wedding experts. You'll choose your music, entertainment, photography and videography, floral arrangements and centerpieces, world-class cuisine for your reception, bride's and groom's cakes, invitations and more.

How much does one of these weddings cost? Well, they have a minimum expenditure of $12,500, but as this book goes to print, this is a typical proposal, based on one hundred guests:

Wedding Ceremony

- Pavilion fee $1,590
- Floral estimate for ceremony/reception   1,590
- Organist   0

- Dove release   200
- Limousine (three hours)   210

Wedding Dinner-Dance

- Dinner food	6,560
- Beverages (open bar)	1,703
- Champagne toast	494
- Wedding cake	820
- Entertainment (DJ)	700
- Characters: Mickey/Minnie	650
Estimated Total	**$14,517**

Note: This total is only an estimate because of the many variables. For example, actual beverage consumption may be higher than estimated. Also, this total does not include all sales tax, gratuities or such items as officiant fees, photography, videography or honeymoon accommodations. It also does not include some of the wonderful options available, such as:

- Horse and carriage $750
- Cinderella's glass coach $2,200
- "Staged Bands"   from $1,750
- Themed decor   from $300
- Harpist, guitarist, violinist, trios
  or quartets $275 to $875
- Airport transport   from $60

It should be noted that all prices stated above were current as this book went to press and are subject to change.

Although these extras can add up, it is still possible to spend less than the national average on the wedding and reception combined, and where else can a bride be a real-life Cinderella for a whole day? It's no wonder this is one of the most popular destination wedding venues in the United States. Order a copy of the Disney's Fairy Tale Wedding video, and you'll understand why!

By the way, if you're interested in being married at Disneyland in Anaheim, California, you should call the member of the Association of Bridal

Consultants who specializes in planning the Disney West Coast wedd will find her information in the appendix, along with other membe specialize in planning weddings in Orlando, Florida.

A Nevada Wedding

Nevada has been a popular wedding state for many years, not only because the wedding license requirements are so lenient, but because there are so many wedding chapels available where a couple can be married on very short notice. Add to this the fact that Lake Tahoe and Las Vegas have traditionally been popular honeymoon destinations, and it is only natural that the wedding industry has flourished.

Here are a few of my favorite wedding chapels in Nevada.

CAL-NEVA LODGE, NORTH SHORE LAKE TAHOE

There are several reasons why I like the Cal-Neva Lodge: The wedding coordinators are experienced and efficient; it is easily accessible, yet tucked away on the North Shore; it is a beautiful facility. But most of all, the outdoor wedding gazebo is stunning! Not only is the ornate, white gazebo exquisite, but the view of Lake Tahoe directly behind it is probably one of the most photographed in the world. Framed by pine trees, tall mountains in the distance reflect off the clear, still lake waters, creating a scene even the finest artist would have difficulty capturing on canvas. In case of inclement weather, you can opt for the intimate Lakeview Chapel, which also has spectacular lake views, or one of the other ceremony settings.

Cal-Neva's wedding department is staffed with three talented personal wedding coordinators who will make all your ceremony, reception and honeymoon arrangements, including:

- Your choice of four ceremony sites, each with services of a minister and a keyboardist
- Floral packages
- Photography and videography
- Reception food, beverages, cake and entertainment
- Tuxedo rentals
- Limousine service

- Rehearsal dinner
- Beauty services
- Health spa services
- Endless Love honeymoon packages starting at $439

Tahoe's marriage license requirements are quite lenient, as I mentioned. There is no blood test or waiting period, but you must appear before the county clerk in Incline Village, where you will be required to furnish valid photo IDs and a $35 fee.

Your personal wedding coordinator will take pride in helping you, guiding you and working with you every step of the way. She will answer your questions, offer suggestions and do everything possible to make your wedding the most joyous and memorable experience of your life.

Here is the story of one couple whose Cal-Neva wedding was perfect in every way.

SUCCESS STORY # 3

Karen and Steve Rakich

Karen, age 38, and Steve, age 41, met through a mutual friend who gave Steve Karen's phone number. Steve called her that very night, and they talked for an hour and a half. He asked if he could take her out to dinner two days later, and Karen accepted. Karen was working in the airline industry and living in Reno at the time, and Steve lived thirty-five miles away in Truckee, California. He is a wild lands firefighter and culturist with the U.S. Forest Service.

They really hit it off on their first date. Obviously, the matchmaking "took," for they started seeing each other all the time.

Meanwhile, Karen's two children by her first marriage, Karmelle, age 15, and Lance, age 12, "fell in love with Steve" and the next thing they knew the children were spending a lot of time with him in Truckee. Eventually, Steve began to "talk marriage," but he wasn't sure how the kids would feel about it until one day he asked them, "How would you like to live here in Truckee and go to school here?"

They jumped at the chance. And then Steve asked how they would like having him as their stepdad, and they were equally elated!

Once Steve felt good about the children's feelings, he formally proposed to Karen later that night in front of a romantic little fire in his wood-burning stove. Karen was absolutely sure he was the right one and, of course, she said, "Yes."

Karen didn't want to get married in Truckee or her hometown of Reno, but she liked the idea of getting married at Lake Tahoe. Steve suggested Cal-Neva at Crystal Bay because he had heard it was really beautiful.

The moment Karen drove into Cal-Neva's parking lot, she was sure this was the site she wanted. The wedding coordinators took her on a tour of the facilities, and Karen was amazed at all the possibilities. Because she had been married before with a traditional church wedding and sit-down dinner reception with over three hundred guests, she thought a smaller wedding might be better this time. Karen's first wedding had made her and her mother "beside ourselves with stress," so she hoped this one would be a little less hectic.

Because this was Steve's first marriage, however, he wanted a traditional wedding, surrounded by their friends and family members, many of whom could hardly believe Steve was finally getting married! They eventually settled on a medium-sized wedding with one hundred guests who would be coming to Cal-Neva from Reno, Truckee, Washington state and other cities in California.

Their wedding was planned for March and Cal-Neva's outdoor wedding gazebo would be closed because of snow, so they chose one of their two indoor chapels, The Lady of the Lake Chapel, which was the perfect size for their one hundred guests.

To give you an idea how stress-free this wedding was to plan compared to Karen's first, all these choices were made in one easy visit with Cal-Neva's wedding coordinators: the selection of the chapel, minister, keyboardist, reception room, photographer, videographer, floral package, food and drink, tuxedos, wedding cake and their honeymoon. All this in less than an hour!

After this one brief meeting, the only thing Karen had left to do was shop for her wedding gown and her attendants' dresses. She went to The Wedding Shop in Reno, walked over to the rack of new arrivals, saw a dress she loved, tried it on and bought it! Her attendants met her there a week later, and their gowns were chosen just as quickly.

When I asked Karen about her wedding day, she said, "It couldn't have been easier or more perfect—the wedding coordinators saw to it that everything ran smoothly. There isn't a book big enough to hold our feelings and thoughts and all our thank-yous to the Cal-Neva wedding staff. It was outstanding from start to finish!" ♡

THE WEDDING CHAPEL AT CAESARS, SOUTH SHORE LAKE TAHOE

This wedding chapel is the newest wedding facility at Lake Tahoe and blends majestic Roman architecture with twenty-first-century conveniences. Its most delightful feature is a raised marble altar backlighted with a glowing sunset, mystical moonlight or the brilliance of a blue sky.

Depending on the number of guests and the day of the week, chapel rental rates start at $65 and include complimentary prerecorded music and use of one of their elegant bridal finishing rooms. Everything else is extra, although quite reasonably priced:

- Minister's fee—a minimum cash donation of $40
- Unity candle ceremony—additional $15
- Live musical packages beginning at $55
- Photography packages beginning at $120
- Videography packages beginning at $155
- Floral packages beginning at $60

Other extras include the services of a full-service beauty salon, reception buffets, sit-down dinners or luncheons, wedding cake and a cruise on Lake Tahoe's crystal blue waters.

TREASURE ISLAND, LAS VEGAS

Treasure Island at the Mirage is the place to get married and spend your honeymoon if you're looking for something fun and different. It is billed as "The idyllic pirate's getaway in the desert," and it certainly is that—a fun, adventurous theme resort. In fact, from the moment you approach Treasure

Island, you find yourself transported to an eighteenth-century bustling Caribbean pirate village that features, among other things, a pyrotechnic battle to the finish with cannons firing, ammunition exploding and stuntmen flying through the air into the waters below. (The pirates win, of course!)

Amidst all this fun and fantasy, Treasure Island offers two graciously appointed wedding chapels, each with marble-lined altars, exquisite floral arrangements and elegant decor. Professional wedding coordinators arrange all the wedding details, including rental of wedding attire for the bride, groom and the members of the wedding party, bouquets and boutonnieres, photography and videography, rehearsal dinner, cocktail reception or dinner-dance, custom-designed wedding cake, entertainment, custom-designed floral arrangements, invitations, matchbooks, napkins, calligraphy and mailing, hair stylist, manicurist, gifts for the wedding party, party favors, officiant, wedding music, a bottle of champagne and, of course, honeymoon accommodations.

They will customize any wedding, or the bride and groom may choose from these wedding packages:

- Silver Treasures ($379): wedding ceremony, bride's and groom's flowers, photos (two 8″×10″, four 5″×7″, six wallets)
- Gold Treasures ($499): wedding ceremony, bride's and groom's flowers, photos (one 11″×14″, three 8″×10″, four 5″×7″, six wallets), videotape of the ceremony
- Diamond Treasures ($599): same as Gold Treasures, except the photo package is a little more elaborate
- Pearl Treasures ($799): similar to Diamond Treasures, plus champagne flutes and a deluxe room for one night
- Platinum Treasures ($1,399): similar to Pearl Treasures, plus a Beautiful Bride Spa Package and Handsome Groom Spa Package

Treasure Island also has various dinner buffet, sit-down dinner and brunch buffet packages, plus various optional extras, such as porcelain bride and groom or pearl-handle cake knives.

Las Vegas marriage license requirements are quite lenient: no proof of divorce, blood test or waiting period required, and the fee is only $35.

Over 100,000 couples get married in Las Vegas every year (that's one every five minutes!) in hundreds of wedding chapels throughout the city, but what impresses me about the chapels at Treasure Island is their elegance. They were obviously designed, decorated and furnished on an "unlimited budget"—topiary trees, oak pews, exquisite carpeting, wallpaper and wall hangings and impressive raised altar setting. Lovely!

A couple of notes about Las Vegas weddings: First of all, any prices quoted above are current as this book goes to print but are subject to change. Second, if you would like to hire an independent bridal consultant to plan your Las Vegas wedding, I have listed several in the appendix who are members of the Association of Bridal Consultants.

A Poconos Wedding
CAESARS POCONO RESORTS

Every one of Caesars Pocono Resorts, located in northeastern Pennsylvania, offers Caesars Secret Rendezvous Weddings in conjunction with a minimum two-night honeymoon stay. Each resort has a full-time wedding coordinator who will help you tour the property to choose the romantic ceremony setting of your choice and make all your arrangements.

Caesars' wedding package includes the ceremony, performed by a local officiant; his and hers wedding T-shirts; sparkling or spirit-free champagne toast; designer champagne glasses for the bride and groom; wedding photo album; eight 5" × 7" color photographs and a small wedding cake—all for a total cost of only $325, which is subject to change, of course, at any time.

Pennsylvania state marriage license law is fairly lenient, requiring the couple to appear in person at least three days prior to the wedding date with proof of identity, a birth certificate and/or driver's license, blood test results and original divorce decree, if applicable. The blood tests may be obtained in your home state, but the results must be recorded on a Pennsylvania Department of Health Form, which can be mailed to you in advance by one of Caesars' wedding coordinators.

You can choose from any of these locations for your honeymoon stay: Cove Haven, Paradise Stream, Pocono Palace or Brookdale, each with its own personality.

Cove Haven, located on Lake Wallenpaupack, is considered to be a ravishingly elegant showcase of world-class entertainment, exquisite dining and state-of-the-art facilities of every conceivable kind. There are indoor and outdoor pools, a health club and spa, indoor ice skating and roller-skating, water skiing, tennis, snowmobiling, bicycling, nearby snow skiing and a spectacular million-dollar nightclub.

Paradise Stream, surrounded by a winding stream, is the coziest of all the resorts and offers many of the same amenities as Cove Haven.

Pocono Palace boasts a grand country-club style that oozes with Roman ambience. Located on a secluded 430-acre estate, you can enjoy golf near a beautiful lake, as well as the new 32,000-square-foot indoor arena featuring all kinds of indoor sports, including tennis, racquetball and billiards.

Brookdale, also on a large wooded estate with a private lake, is known for its private villas and cottages.

Each location has its own allure, and it's difficult to choose among them, which is why, no matter where you actually bed down each night, all activities at all four locations are available in your one all-inclusive honeymoon package.

Depending on which resort you choose and how far you must travel, their "air-inclusive" package rates run from about $1,800 to $2,300 per couple for six days, five nights. For example, if you were flying from Los Angeles and staying in a Fairway Suite at the Pocono Palace, the total cost would be about $2,250 per couple. This includes your air fare; daily breakfast, dinner, hors d'oeuvres and late-night snacks; and all of the sports activities and entertainment available at their four locations. If you add the cost of the wedding package, you'll still be way under $3,000 for everything, even if you're flying in from the West Coast! Such a deal! And totally worry-free.

A Mountain Wedding

Not every couple dreams of a glitz-and-glamour wedding and honeymoon, cavorting with Mickey Mouse, playing games with the "one-armed bandits" or bobbing nude by the hour in a sensuous hot tub. Many couples actually prefer a rustic mountain setting where they can feel close to nature.

Two such settings are Mountain Valley Chapel in Pigeon Forge, Tennessee, and Teton Mountain Weddings in Jackson Hole, Wyoming. As I researched these incredible sites, I was very fortunate to uncover two touching love stories, which are also included here.

MOUNTAIN VALLEY CHAPEL, PIGEON FORGE, TENNESSEE

Located on an eighteen-acre parcel just outside Pigeon Forge, Mountain Valley Chapel is constructed of cedar and glass and is surrounded by awesome views of the Great Smoky Mountains. The sanctuary seats about one hundred and is famous for its floor-to-ceiling windows. This magnificent chapel offers a Christian wedding ceremony performed in candlelight by an ordained minister.

Several full-time wedding coordinators plan absolutely everything, including all details of the ceremony, reception and the couple's honeymoon stay in one of the honeymoon log cabins located on the property. Although the coordinators will plan a customized wedding of the couple's choice, there are six convenient wedding packages from which to choose. For example, The Diamond Radiance includes:

- Formal portraits matted in a gold-embossed wedding album, plus a 16″×20″ portrait on canvas
- A unity candle service
- Videotape of the ceremony
- Bridal bouquet, groom's boutonniere and bride's garter, plus flowers for other members of the wedding party
- Beauty services for the bride (hair stylist, makeup artist and manicurist)
- Tuxedos for the groom, his groomsmen, ring bearer, ushers and participating family members
- Extended limousine service
- A reception following the ceremony that includes a tiered wedding cake and a professional disc jockey who provides music for up to four hours
- Honeymoon accommodations for three nights
- Tickets to a local theater for the wedding couple
- A romantic candlelight dinner for two

Mountain Valley's other wedding services vary according to how many of these amenities are included. The optional Family Medallion Service includes a meaningful addition to the ceremony when children are involved. After the traditional exchange of wedding vows and rings, the children are invited to join the bride and groom. After some quiet words spoken by the minister about the children and the special relationships they will bring into this new family, the couple places a Family Medallion around the neck of each child as they pledge to love and support the children. Very touching!

I should mention that the state of Tennessee has very "friendly" marriage laws in that there are no blood or medical tests required, and there is no waiting period involved with the marriage license process. Brides and grooms who arrive from other states can visit the local courthouse and quickly acquire a marriage license for a fee of $36.

The lenient marriage laws are only one reason brides and grooms flock to Pigeon Forge to be married, however; the main reason is that the entire Pigeon Forge–Gatlinburg area is such a wholesome, fun place to spend a honeymoon. Here are just a few of the reasons why:

- Absolutely gorgeous mountain setting
- Home of dozens of live theaters, including the Louise Mandrell Theater, Memories Theater, Dollywood's Music Mansion Theater, the Comedy Barn, the Eagle Mountain Theater, the Dixie Stampede Dinner Theatre, the Tennessee Music Theater and the Smoky Mountain Jubilee, just to name a few
- Home of Winterfest, which includes millions of twinkling lights, frolicking bears, Victorian skaters, and so forth, and Wilderness Wildlife Week of Nature (walks, talks and seminars amidst the beauty of the Great Smoky Mountains)
- Fabulous restaurants, including the Alabama Grill, established by country singing group Alabama, and Alan Jackson's Showcar Cafe
- Over two hundred factory outlet stores that draw tourists from all over the southeast
- Tennessee's #1 attraction: Dollywood, a theme park with one-of-a-kind attractions and special events

I have only scratched the surface here, but you get the idea. It's no wonder so many couples come to Pigeon Forge to get married and spend their honeymoon!

And now here's one of those love stories I promised you.

Christy and Adam Durrett

Christy and Adam Durrett were married at Mountain Valley Chapel in Pigeon Forge after a fifteen-month courtship.

Adam was in the Marine Corps and Christy was a student at the University of North Carolina when they met through a mutual friend on April 29, 1995. They both were twenty-one at the time, and they hit it off right away; in fact, Christy knew she wanted to marry Adam from Day One, but it took Adam a little longer to realize they were meant for each other—two whole weeks!

Adam's formal wedding proposal—on November 19 of that same year—was *intended* to be an incredibly romantic moment. At least, that was the way he had it planned! He drove Christy to his parents' home, where he planned to propose to her down by the lake in back of the house. Adam said, "I sort of designed her ring myself," and he had planned to say some very tender, romantic words of love as he presented it to her.

Well, the moon was reflecting off the lake, and the moment couldn't have been more precious except for one thing: Christy was freezing cold, and even though Adam gave her his jacket, she continued to tremble and jump around in an effort to warm up. Because Christy was such a frozen jumping jack and couldn't stand still long enough for Adam to deliver his romantic soliloquy, he cut his speech to these four words, "Will you marry me?"

Once they were formally engaged, they began to talk about what kind of ceremony they wanted and where they wanted to be married. Two things they knew from the start: They wanted to get married in a unique and special place, and they wanted a spiritual, Christian wedding. They also wanted their close friends and family members present, but choosing a location was difficult because their guests would be traveling from Texas, South Carolina, North Carolina, Georgia, Iowa,

Michigan, Kansas, Kentucky, Illinois, New Jersey, New York and Paris, France.

One day as they happened to be driving through Pigeon Forge, Tennessee, it hit them! What a perfect place to get married—not only because they could be married in a Christian service on top of a mountain, but because Pigeon Forge was halfway between her family and his. They also felt that the Pigeon Forge–Gatlinburg area would be a great place for their friends and family to meet and have a lot of fun together after Adam and Christy left on their honeymoon to the Bahamas. So, although most couples come to Pigeon Forge for their wedding *and* honeymoon, Adam and Christy chose the setting because it would provide a fun vacation for their guests after the wedding.

The wedding coordinators at Mountain Valley Chapel took care of all the wedding and reception arrangements, including:

- Furnishing a minister (who co-officiated the service with Adam's uncle, a Baptist minister)
- Flowers and decorations
- Music
- Reception food for seventy-five guests
- Wedding cake
- Photography and videography
- Hair stylist, makeup artist and manicurist
- All-day limousine service
- Rental of seven tuxes
- Guest book
- A two-night stay at Chapel Mountain Cabins, which are located on the eighteen-acre property
- Reserving a block of rooms for the guests

The only things Christy took care of were the selection of her wedding gown and her bridesmaids' gowns and the invitations, although the Mountain Valley staff would have taken care of the invitations, too, if the couple would have preferred.

"Everything I asked for, she (the wedding coordinator) did for us. It was so great for me because I knew everything was being taken care of," stated Christy, who told me the grand total of $6,500 was well worth it, considering everything that was included.

All the planning really paid off because the wedding and reception went off without a single glitch—that is, except for one *tiny* thing: Adam's groomsmen tossed him into the swimming pool at the reception site, which wouldn't have been a problem except that his pockets were full of bills from the "Dollar Dance." Evidently the limousine that transported them to the airport after the reception was a pretty funny sight: $1,500 in dripping wet bills spread all over the seats in the hopes they would dry before they arrived at the airport. No such luck! They ended up stuffing the wet bills into a plastic bag that they carried with them onto the plane.

Oh, well—the warm Caribbean breezes probably dried them out in no time and I'm sure they were lots of fun to spend! ♡

TETON NATIONAL PARK

Teton Mountain Weddings in Jackson Hole, Wyoming, arranges everything, from the simplest lakeside ceremony surrounded by the majestic Tetons to the rustic elegance of a beautiful lodge. They even make arrangements for flights, lodging and activities, such as horseback adventures in the backcountry, covered wagon rides, chuckwagon dinners, rodeos, snowmobiling, jeep trips, sleigh rides, river rafting, mountain climbing, skiing, music concerts, hot air balloon races or an antique car show. The wedding night and honeymoon can be spent in one of Jackson Hole's beautiful lodges with a cozy fireplace or a Jacuzzi in the room.

Karen Brody, owner of Teton Mountain Weddings, is an interfaith minister who performs many of the marriage ceremonies herself. These nuptials take place in mountain meadows, along riversides, in log chapels, or at the end of a horseback or snowmobile ride.

Most of the couples who marry in the Tetons have been married before and don't want another traditional wedding. Karen said, "Most are in their thirties or forties and want something different, something personalized."

A prime example of "something different" is the "dogsled wedding." A dogsled wedding consists of an entire day. Everyone leaves from a point about twenty miles south of Jackson Hole, two people to a sled. If you are able, you can "mush" and drive your own team, along with a guide. The trip is about twelve miles through a forest, along frozen streams to a hot spring where there is a rustic cabin that is used to change into bathing suits. Then you enjoy the splendor of soaking in the hot springs while the guides prepare lunch, which consists of steak or trout served picnic style under snow-covered trees—truly amazing. The wedding ceremony itself can take place at the hot springs or somewhere along the way.

Karen takes care of everything, including flowers, lodging, photographer, music, special use permits for the national parks, reception and cake—she even escorts the couple to the courthouse for their marriage license, which costs $25. When you read the success story below, you'll get an idea of just how complete her services really are!

Jackson Hole, Grand Teton and Yellowstone National Parks are glorious honeymoon destinations. I'm sure there is no more beautiful place in the world—definitely one of my personal favorites.

SUCCESS STORY # 5

Rhonda and Tim Jackson

Rhonda and Tim Jackson were married on June 15, 1996, as they stood on the shore of String Lake in Wyoming's Teton National Park. Their wedding was arranged by Karen Brody of Teton Mountain Weddings. If you're thinking of a western theme for your wedding, you're going to love this story.

Rhonda and Tim were both on the brink of turning thirty when they met at a birthday party for a mutual friend. Rhonda's first impression of Tim was that "he was sooooo cute—looked just like Alan Jackson, with his blond hair and mustache." They started dating and within a month they knew they loved each other. Tim officially proposed to Rhonda about nine months later, although he had been hinting at marriage for quite a while with comments like, "When we get married . . ."

One day, after one of these comments, Rhonda told him, "What do you mean 'when we get married'? I've never been asked, and until I've been asked I don't know whose marriage you're talking about."

Tim was quiet for about fifteen minutes and then he said, "Well, do you wanna?"

Rhonda replied, "Do I wanna what?"

And Tim said, "Well, you know—do you wanna?"

She said, "I don't know what you mean."

Finally Tim made it clear: "You know—do you wanna get married?"

She teasingly hemmed and hawed for a while until finally saying, "Yes." Then she asked him what kind of wedding he'd like to have, and he said he wanted to "get married on the side of a mountain in my cowboy boots."

Well, a year later they *both* wore cowboy boots, along with the rest of their western wedding attire, as they said "I do" in a pristine wilderness setting with the Grand Tetons in the distance. Rhonda's gown was a simple white off-the-shoulder trimmed with fringed top and bottom, topped by her white cowboy hat with lace and ribbons that hung down her back.

Her maid of honor wore a "Miss Kitty" saloon girl gown of fuchsia and black. Both gowns had been rented ahead of time from Marlene's in Fond du Lac, Wisconsin, a store that carries over 25,000 period costumes.

Tim and his best man purchased their outfits. Tim wore black jeans, a white tux shirt, a waist-length western tux jacket, cowboy hat and, *of course*, his cowboy boots. His best man dressed the same, except that he wore a black vest instead of a jacket.

Twenty-seven friends and family members drove from three states to attend the wedding, mostly in their 4×4 pickup trucks. Every guest was provided with a corsage or boutonniere that had been created from silk flowers entwined with rope by one of the bride's girlfriends, who also fashioned Rhonda's bouquet.

The only fresh flowers purchased locally was a large bouquet of native wildflowers, which contributed to a very touching addition to the ceremony. Tim and Rhonda carried the bouquet to the edge of the lake and cast the flowers onto the water in memory of two precious people in their lives who had died: the bride's brother and one of Tim and Rhonda's close friends. As the guests witnessed this poignant tribute, there wasn't a dry eye—as you can imagine.

What impresses me about Tim and Rhonda's wedding is not only the simple purity of the ceremony itself and the awesome ambience of the setting, but the way the western theme repeated itself throughout. It all began the night before the wedding when a caravan of covered wagons carried them and their guests up into the mountains for a chuckwagon dinner, which doubled as their rehearsal dinner. Along the way they were "attacked" by Indians and greeted by mountain men. When they finally arrived at the site of the chuckwagon dinner, they were entertained by cowboy comedians and singers.

The reception was held at Jackson Hole Golf and Tennis Club in a restaurant called the Strutting Grouse where the guests ate appetizers and drank champagne during the couple's photo session, followed by a dinner of salmon, filet mignon, polenta and grilled vegetables. The wedding cake was in the shape of a horseshoe with a western caketop they had brought with them: a little cowboy and cowgirl lassoed together with a rope.

After the reception everyone went to the rodeo with the wedding party still dressed in their wedding garb. This drew attention, of course, and soon they were celebrities. Rhonda said people were yelling "congratulations" from the stands and then gave them a standing ovation. After the rodeo, the evening was topped off with a trip to a local country-western bar where the band played songs especially for them. Finally, at midnight, Tim and Rhonda said goodbye to everyone and headed for their honeymoon bed at Jackson Hole Lodge.

When I asked Rhonda if there was anything she would have done differently, this is what she said:

"Diane, there is nothing I would have changed about the entire day. Karen took care of everything—she was the best. It was absolutely a hassle-free wedding." ♡

Other Destinations

This was my personal list of favorite destination wedding venues; obviously, there are hundreds more scattered all over the country. If you have a certain honeymoon site in mind and the idea of a destination wedding sounds interesting, call the chamber of commerce or visitor's bureau in the area you are considering. Also, check with your travel agent, who will help you locate a venue where you can be married without all the hassles.

Finally, if the honeymoon resort you choose doesn't offer the services of a personal wedding coordinator, you may need help from a professional bridal consultant who plans weddings near your honeymoon destination. To locate one who is ethical and knowledgeable, call the Association of Bridal Consultants who will refer you to one of their members. The association number is listed in the appendix, along with references to those members who specialize in planning destination weddings in Arkansas, Connecticut, Disneyland in California, Florida, Idaho, Las Vegas, the mountains of Colorado, South Carolina, Tennessee and Vermont.

Good luck!

THINGS TO REMEMBER:

○ All-inclusive honeymoon packages include the gratuities, so don't feel guilty about leaving the dinner table without leaving a tip.

○ Let the natural ambience of your relaxed, carefree honeymoon setting set the tone for your destination wedding.

○ When booking your accommodations, you can save a lot of money by opting for a room with a garden view instead of an ocean view. Trust me—honeymoon couples don't spend much time looking out the window anyway!

○ Any friends or family members who come along are responsible for their own transportation and lodging costs. But remember, don't invite a crowd or the wedding will no longer be "worry-free."

○ Wedding announcements can be mailed any time after your honeymoon.

○ READ THE FINE PRINT IN ALL CONTRACTS BEFORE SIGNING!

CHAPTER THREE

The Destination Wedding Outside Mainland U.S.

Weddings are becoming more and more commonplace at honeymoon sites around the world, the most popular of which are in the Caribbean, Mexico, Hawaii and the South Pacific. It has also become quite trendy to be married aboard a cruise liner before setting sail or at one of their points of embarkation.

In this chapter I have listed my favorite sites in the most popular venues outside mainland United States. In order to qualify for this list, the sites had to pass the same four tests I mentioned in the last chapter:

1. Offer all-inclusive packages that include the services of an experienced, well-qualified wedding coordinator
2. Have a romantic setting
3. Have an excellent reputation
4. Have uncomplicated marriage license requirements

My list is by no means intended to be a complete directory of destination wedding possibilities, but only some of my personal favorites that may whet your appetite for the delicious advantages of this concept. Any prices quoted are, of course, subject to change.

Hawaii

I have been to Hawaii seven times, and it's obvious to me why it is the number-one destination wedding choice for couples who want to be married at their honeymoon sites. Although the islands vary in their romantic appeal, I'm not one of those picky travelers who puts Oahu down for its "commercialism," or Kauai for its "limited recreational facilities," or the big island of Hawaii for its "vast starkness." I think each island is gorgeous and romantic and wonderful in its own way and certainly a far cry from life in our own hometowns.

So, which island is the best choice for a destination wedding? It depends on your personal preferences. If you're looking for a quiet, secluded setting where you can just enjoy each other and not be bothered by the crowds, you may choose the big island. If you're looking for an abundance of flora and fauna, you may prefer the garden isle, Kauai. Or, if you're on a tight budget, Oahu is definitely the right choice for you because it is the most affordable. If, however, money isn't a problem and you want the typical picture-perfect-postcard setting, with swaying palms, white sand beaches and plenty of things to see and do, you'll probably choose the most popular island when it comes to destination weddings—Maui.

Here are some of the easiest, most worry-free destination wedding venues I've found in Hawaii.

FOUR SEASONS RESORT MAUI AT WAILEA

This fairly new resort—opened in 1990—is opulent beyond belief and has received a five diamond AAA rating. Located on fifteen acres in Wailea along Maui's southwestern coast, this plantation-styled resort has received rave reviews for its exquisite amenities, including its enormous swimming pools, Jacuzzis, fountains, profusion of blooming orchids and tropical plants, waterfalls, golf courses, beach walks, tennis courts, health club, snorkeling, scuba diving, sailing instruction, limo champagne picnic lunches, dining options and renowned pampering by their staff. (They even come by and spray you with a cool mist to keep you comfortable as you bake in the sun.)

The Four Seasons Resort Maui offers several honeymoon packages, ranging from approximately $1,400 per couple for a three-night stay, to a seven-night romance package at about $4,000 that includes limo transfer, an ocean-view room, champagne, bathrobes, dinner for two, limo picnic with champagne and the use of a convertible.

The Four Seasons Resort Maui is one of the most popular destination wedding sites in all of Hawaii, not only because it is such an incredible honeymoon spot, but also because of the array of photogenic ceremony settings, such as the Seasons Garden, the Sculpture Gardens and a grassy knoll above the ocean. Wedding packages range from the Plumeria Wedding at about $1,000, which includes the ceremony, leis, solo musician and a bottle of champagne, to the Lokelani Wedding, priced at less than $2,000. The Lokelani is a popular choice for the couple who prefers a more elaborate affair that includes a wedding cake, additional flowers and a couple of other extras.

Of course, the *real* beauty of this whole idea is that all the planning is done for you by one of their experienced coordinators who will even wrap your wedding and honeymoon into one worry-free package. And unless you really have your heart set on bringing your wedding gown with you on the plane, you can do what so many couples do—purchase native Hawaiian wedding attire after you arrive.

THE HALEKULANI ON WAIKIKI BEACH

Even though this luxury resort is situated in the middle of the busy hubbub of Waikiki, it has an amazingly tranquil five-acre oceanfront setting and has received excellent reviews by critics around the world, including *Lifestyles of the Rich and Famous*. It definitely qualifies as "romantic" with its balconies that overlook the sea, sensual Hawaiian music that floats up from the beach below, and the moonlit walks along the beach.

The Halekulani offers many amenities, including world-class restaurants, breakfast served in your private lanai, flowers and French champagne, a gift of his and hers cotton bathrobes, a glorious oceanside swimming pool and all kinds of water sports: outrigger canoes, surfing, snorkeling, deep-sea fishing and windsurfing.

I highly recommend this resort for water-loving couples whose idea of heaven is spending the day on the ocean. Then, if you have energy left over, you can enjoy Waikiki's exciting night life with its luaus, musical performers, comedians and native Hawaiian dancing.

The Halekulani's honeymoon packages range from $1,429 for four days, three nights to their Heaven on Waikiki Honeymoon, which includes eight days, seven nights for about $3,000.

Although the Halekulani doesn't offer package wedding plans per se, it does take care of everything, including a marriage license and a minister, which can usually be arranged within twenty-four hours. The Halekulani's coordinators pride themselves on their ability to personalize each wedding, which normally takes place in an enchanting on-site wedding gazebo.

You can purchase your wedding attire after you arrive or rent your gown from one of several bridal gown rental shops within easy walking distance of the Halekulani.

It's all so easy!

HYATT REGENCY KAUAI RESORT

Love to surf? This resort may be for you. It is located on fifty acres along Kauai's south shore on the sunny side of the island. Situated on Shipwreck Beach, it is popular with surfers because of its prime surf strand.

The resort has the feel of an old Hawaiian sugarcane plantation—quiet and relaxed, with a "hang-loose attitude" about it. If you love the water, but you're not into surfing, there are five acres of swimming lagoons with a gentle three-miles-per-hour current to carry you along. Or, if you like more action, you can try out the twisting water slide that zips you from top to bottom in half a blink.

Orchids bloom absolutely everywhere, and there are four excellent restaurants, a Robert Trent Jones II–designed golf course, four tennis courts and the Anara Spa, famous for its Royal Hawaiian Facial.

Honeymoon rates start at about $285 per couple per night, depending on the time of year, in addition to a variety of wedding packages that range from about $1,000 to $2,000. Over two hundred couples a year choose the Hyatt Regency Kauai as their destination wedding site. The resort has a wedding department that handles all the arrangements, including many special island touches, such as flower leis, a conch-shell blower and, of course, plenty of that romantic Hawaiian music. They will even make arrangements for a replica of an award-winning holoku gown for the bride, which is the traditional Hawaiian wedding gown.

This is definitely a tempting hassle-free Hawaiian venue to consider.

AMERICAN HAWAII CRUISES

This cruise line is famous for its onboard Nani Kai ("Beautiful Seas") Wedding Package which includes the services of a wedding coordinator, an officiant to perform the ceremony, Hawaiian-style music performed by onboard musicians, a delicate flower lei and haku (floral headpiece) for the bride, a flower lei or boutonniere for the groom, photography service, souvenir wedding photo album, two-tiered wedding cake, chilled champagne and his and hers fluted champagne glasses. All this for a package price of around $600. A cocktail reception or elegant wedding buffet is extra, the price depending on the number of guests you bring on board.

This package is only available to the ship's passengers and takes place on the bridge of the ship or, if you bring a large wedding party along, at another location on board.

Before boarding the ship the bride and groom must appear in person before the Marriage License Bureau of Hawaii. The license is pretty easy to get except for one small thing: The bride must produce a certificate from her U.S. or Canadian doctor stating that she has been immunized for rubella. If she hasn't, she will be required to pass a rubella blood test which can be performed at home beforehand. A two-day precruise stay is recommended to allow ample time to obtain the marriage license.

If you'd like to be married in Hawaii, but your honeymoon site wasn't mentioned here, call the concierge at your resort to ask if the staff arranges weddings. If not, you may want to consult with a member of the Association of Bridal Consultants who lives in Hawaii and specializes in Hawaiian weddings; I have listed several in the appendix.

Fiji

If Hawaii is a little too touristy for what you have in mind, you may want to consider Fiji, one of the most exotic, unspoiled, romantic honeymoon settings to be found anywhere in the world. In fact, if you really want to get away from it all—career pressures, nagging relatives, honking horns, doorbells and message machines—this is *definitely* the place for you!

It's no wonder there are 167 resorts on the islands of Fiji, and it's also not surprising that Fiji's popularity as a destination wedding choice has increased by 200 percent in the past couple of years.

The South Seas charm of these relaxed, "untouristy" islands is evident everywhere you go, whether strolling down a remote, palm-studded beach or being welcomed by the warm, loving Fijian people, who still live the simple life, as they have for many centuries.

NAMALE RESORT, FIJI

Namale Resort is a secluded 121-acre sanctuary, tucked in and around lava rocks, surrounded by lush rain forests. Owned by Tony Robbins and his wife, Becky, it is also one of the country's least expensive all-inclusive resorts. You have probably heard of Tony—he is a best-selling author, television star and peak performance coach.

What makes Namale so special is its magical "out-of-this-world" ambience, created not only by the native grace and majesty of the facilities themselves, but by the prehistoric natural beauty of the island and the love and warmth of the Fijian staff and local villagers. It's very difficult to describe in words—and believe me, I'm trying—but let me put it this way: If you can imagine a place that's diametrically opposed to Manhattan's Fifth Avenue at rush hour, this is it!

The Namale Resort has several all-inclusive honeymoon packages to choose from that include private accommodations in a luxury *bure* (thatched-roof cottage), full-service breakfasts, lunches, snacks, hors d'oeuvres and dinners, round-trip transfers to and from Savusavu airport, daily laundry service and dozens of activities. You can relax around the freshwater swimming pool; laze along the beach; snorkel; hike; water-ski; sail; wind surf; play tennis; volleyball or basketball; go canoeing, kayaking or horseback riding or visit the local village—and everything is included in the price.

As a matter of fact, as this book goes to print, they are offering a special package that not only includes a five-night all-inclusive stay, but round-trip airfare from Los Angeles, as well. It is priced at $2,678 per person, double occupancy.

In addition to the honeymoon packages, the Namale also offers several wedding packages, from a simple ceremony for $330, which includes the marriage license, officiant, and flowers for the bride and groom, to a more elaborate traditional ceremony for $975, which also includes champagne, complete wedding setup, Fijian band, traditional Fijian Kava ceremony, wedding cake and the Meke (traditional Fijian dance).

Optional expenses include a wedding video, photographic services and a traditional Fijian wedding costume.

It's very easy to get married in Fiji. All you need are your passport and birth certificate, plus divorce papers if you've been married before. Fijian weddings are legally recognized in the United States, New Zealand and Australia.

The staff at Namale Resort takes care of everything and all you have to do is relax and "experience the moment." Their weddings are as worry-free as you can get, and here is a success story that proves it.

SUCCESS STORY # 6

Tom and Anne Esterquest

I've heard a lot of love stories through the years, and I thought I'd heard it all—until I came upon the love story of Anne Barry and Tom Esterquest. I had chills as I heard how they met, fell in love and were married—with only three days' notice—at Namale Resort in Fiji while attending a seminar there together. As Anne described their wedding to me, she said: "It was the most *beautiful, incredible, magical* wedding."

I agree—it was the closest thing to a modern day fairy tale that I'll probably ever see. Not only because of the magical enchantment of the setting, or because of the "rightness" of it in a human sense, but because of the deep spiritual meaning behind it all.

To convey the full impact of this Cinderella story, let me back up a minute and tell you how Tom and Anne met. They were both in their thirties and well-established in their careers. Tom had been working in Chicago with Anne's brother, Tim, for nine years while Anne worked in her family's business in Houston, Texas. For years Anne had been hearing from her brother about "the illustrious Tom Esterquest," but she had never met him.

One December Tim invited Anne to fly to Chicago to attend his company's Christmas party. He told her, "You've got to come because Tom Esterquest is going to be there, and I want you two to meet."

She was reluctant at first, but when her brother bought her airline ticket, what could she do? She went. And her brother was right. It was love at first sight. Anne said, "When I met Tom, I knew I was home."

Tom felt it too, and the day after they met he told her, "I really think we should work on this relationship to see what is or isn't there." So, she made several return trips to see him again, and within three weeks she was a "goner." On Valentine's Day he proposed and ten months later they were married in Fiji. Although they were engaged and did plan to marry soon, their Fijian wedding was completely spontaneous, inspired by many things—the love and spirituality of the Fijian people, the indescribable beauty of the setting and revelations gleaned from the seminar itself.

In addition to Tom and Anne, about fifty others attended the seminar, entitled "Date with Destiny," which was led by Tony Robbins. During the course of this several-day seminar, the attendees examined their own values, goals and spirituality, culminating finally in the writing of individual "mission statements." The seminar drew out feelings and emotions that hadn't been examined before, resulting in a touching closeness within the group.

Near the end of the seminar Tom felt a tugging in his heart—he wanted to marry Anne there at Namale in the presence of their friends before the seminar was over. But he wanted to surprise Anne with the news, so he confided in Tony Robbins, who made the announcement in front of the entire group. Tony told everyone that Tom and Anne would be married in three days and they were all invited to the wedding!

Well, you can imagine Anne's reaction! She was stunned and touched and thrilled—all at the same time. And, because she had felt the same tug in her own heart, she knew it was meant to be, not only because of what they had learned about themselves during the seminar, but for other reasons as well.

For one thing, they were both affected by the warmth and spirituality of the Fijian people. They sensed it as they attended a Fijian Methodist church service together and later as they mingled with the locals whose hearts were full of joy and love, even though they are very poor by American standards.

And then there was the setting, which also prodded their decision. Anne said, "I never felt so connected with the naturalness of becoming man and wife."

Well, once Tony made the surprise announcement, the staff at Namale pulled all the plans together in three days, whipping up a delectable wedding cake and reception feast. The Methodist minister from the local church was happy to perform the ceremony; Tony and his wife, Becky, agreed to be witnesses; the local villagers were more than eager to sing, entertain, decorate and fashion authentic Fijian wedding attire for the couple.

Tom wore a traditional warrior costume, which consisted of a skirt of leaves, bands of leaves tied around his upper arms and ankles and several leis made from shells and loops of woven tree bark interlaced with fresh flowers. His chest was bare except for the leis—very masculine!

Anne borrowed a white Latex body suit that was wrapped with a white-on-white fabric that flowed to the ground. A side slit revealed a garter made of straw, beads and flowers. She, too, wore the native shell-and-flower leis, plus a crown of flowers on her head.

During the ceremony the minister explained how God is the only source of a happy marriage. The Fijian choir sang hymns, and the couple took part in the sacred Fijian Kava ceremony where they drank the Kava drink together from a coconut shell.

Finally, with only the sounds of the singing birds and crashing surf in the background, Tom and Anne exchanged gifts—another Fijian ritual—which required that each explain the gift's meaning as it was given. Tom gave Anne a small woven bird that had been given to him as a gift by one of the Fijian children when he arrived on the island, and she did likewise, presenting him with a tiny fan shaped like an arrow. Tom explained that the bird symbolized "a Phoenix rising from the ashes." Anne gave Tom her gift with these words: "This arrow symbolizes the new direction you have taken in your life."

Tom and Anne's story—from the day they met in Chicago to their wedding day at Namale resort—is one of the dearest, most poignant I've ever heard. ♡

Mexico
HYATT REGENCY CANCUN, MEXICO

I need to preface my remarks here by saying that this resort came within one paper-thin tortilla of failing my "worry-free" tests.

Yes, it has an experienced, well-qualified wedding coordinator who speaks excellent English.

Yes, it definitely has a romantic setting (you can even be married on the beach).

Yes, it has a superb reputation.

However, uncomplicated marriage license requirements? Not quite, although I "passed" it based on the staff's assurance that all required paperwork can be mailed to the Hyatt's wedding coordinator in advance, who will hand-carry it to the Civil Registry of Cancun and take care of everything for the couple.

According to instructions that were sent to me by Cancun's Civil Registry office, these are the documents you must furnish to obtain a legal marriage certificate:

- Copies of tourist cards
- Copies of birth certificates
- Copies of blood tests
- Copies of passports
- Copies of driver's licenses
- Final divorce decrees (if applicable)
- Names, addresses, ages, nationalities and tourist card numbers of four witnesses
- A completed application that will be furnished by "The Judge"

In addition, a fee must be paid to the cashier at city hall. Finally, the office adds this statement: "Very important. You have to do everything at least a minimum of one month before the wedding date."

When I asked Sulema Duran, Hyatt Regency Cancun's wedding coordinator, about all of these requirements, she assured me that she meets personally with "The Judge" to hand-carry all the paperwork and deliver the application on the couple's behalf. She emphasized the importance of having all the documents to her a couple months before the wedding date to allow time for her to meet with "The Judge." She also said that she and other Hyatt staff members are delighted to serve as a couple's four witnesses, in case the bride and groom don't bring any friends or family members with them.

The Hyatt Regency Cancun doesn't offer "wedding packages" per se because the staff prides itself on customizing each couple's wedding. In fact, the first question Sulema asks the couple is, "What kind of wedding do you envision?" Then she prices out several all-inclusive packages based on the couple's desires and faxes the information to the couple for their approval.

She told me, however, that the least expensive ceremony would cost a minimum of $250 (payment to "The Judge"), plus optional flowers and champagne, although she assured me that she would be happy to arrange for "free decorations."

Other wedding options include any size wedding reception, including decorations and reception food, drink and wedding cake, plus various floral, photography and videography packages. They can also provide the couple's choice of musical entertainment, including a live mariachi or marimba band.

As far as the honeymoon goes, the Hyatt Regency Cancun is a luxury resort hotel that offers all the amenities you would expect: air conditioning, of course, plus beauty salon, fitness center, laundry and valet service, satellite TV, purified water, rental cars, water sports, swimming, several restaurants, live entertainment, nearby shopping and golf. Honeymoon packages start at about $650 for four days, three nights, and include:

- Ocean-view room on one of the exclusive Regency Club floors
- Bottle of champagne
- Welcome fruit basket
- Daily continental breakfast for two
- Cocktails and hors d'oeuvres every evening

- A romantic four-course dinner at the renowned Cilantro Restaurant
- Free massage at the fitness center
- Welcome "Surprise Gift"
- All tips and taxes

Sounds good to me!

Other reputable Mexican resorts that arrange wedding ceremonies are the Casa Turquesa and the Fiesta America Coral Beach, both in Cancun, and La Casa que Canta and Las Brisas, both in Acapulco, where the marriage license requirements are much more lenient, by the way.

In the appendix I have also listed the name of a member of the Association of Bridal Consultants who lives in Mexico City who may be able to help you plan your wedding at a site of your choice.

The Caribbean
CRUISE SHIP WEDDING PACKAGES

The cruise ship wedding packages listed below can be arranged through Cruise Lines, Inc., which represents all major cruise lines sailing in the Caribbean. Its experienced wedding coordinators assure a totally worry-free wedding, whether on board the ship or on shore in St. Thomas.

Here is some general information that applies to all of the packages:
- Ceremonies are usually held on deck, in the ship's library or in one of the lounges.
- Marriage license fees are not included in the prices shown.
- A marriage license application will be sent to you in the mail by the cruise line's wedding coordinator ninety days prior to the wedding date, unless otherwise indicated.
- Blood tests and physical exams are not required unless otherwise indicated.

- Most cruise lines provide an officiant to perform the ceremony, but you may invite your own if he or she is planning to disembark before sailing.
- Family and friends may also attend the ceremony and reception as long as they disembark before sailing.

Carnival Cruise Lines

1. The Basic Wedding ($490): Includes official civil ceremony, taped music, champagne, small wedding cake, bridal bouquet and groom's boutonniere, white bridal aisle, forty-five minutes of photography with no obligation to purchase, and photo album with one 8″ × 10″ portrait.
2. Welcome Aboard Wedding ($950): Includes everything listed for the Basic Wedding, plus a one-hour open bar and hot and cold hors d'oeuvres, two-tiered wedding cake and coffee.
3. Deluxe Romance Wedding ($1,100): Includes all Basic Wedding amenities, plus one-and-a-half-hour reception and an ice carving.
4. On-Island Wedding in St. Thomas, U.S.V.I. ($675): Includes official civil ceremony, choice of locations (beach, waterfall or Blackbeard's Castle), sparkling wine and cake-for-two, music, and photography with no obligation to purchase.

Holland America Line

1. Holland America Wedding ($600): Includes limo transportation, official civil ceremony on board ship, bride's and groom's flowers, champagne and small wedding cake.
2. Shoreside Wedding in St. Thomas ($900): Includes transportation from ship to St. Thomas courthouse to be sworn in for marriage license and transfer to wedding site, official civil ceremony, couple's flowers, mini-reception, champagne and small wedding cake.

Princess Cruises

Princess Cruises does *not* offer wedding services aboard its ships; however, it does offer three wedding packages while docked in St. Thomas.

1. Tropical Paradise ($650): Includes Basic Amenities Package (beach, hillside or garden wedding site), couple's flowers, transportation from the

ship to the site, marriage license fee and two witnesses; choice of clergy, and wedding cake.

2. Elegant Paradise ($1,200): Includes Basic Amenities plus a bottle of Perrier Jouet, two champagne flutes, album with seventy photos and two hours of limo service.

3. Ultimate Paradise ($2,700): Includes Basic Amenities plus a bottle of Dom Perignon, two champagne flutes, videotape of the ceremony, three hours of limo service, and helicopter transportation to a private island for a picnic lunch.

Norwegian Cruise Line

1. Petite Cruise Ship Wedding ($225): Covers official civil ceremony at your choice of shipboard locations.

2. Classic Cruise Ship Wedding ($499): Covers official civil ceremony on board ship or in port in Miami or Ft. Lauderdale, bouquet of silk flowers and wedding album containing twenty-four photos.

Majesty Cruise Line

1. Pearl Wedding ($375): Covers ceremony with notary public and witnesses, champagne and wedding certificate.

2. Sapphire Wedding ($425): Same as above, plus crystal flutes.

3. Ruby Wedding ($525): Same as Sapphire, plus wedding cake.

4. Emerald Wedding ($650): Same as Ruby, plus larger wedding cake and a keepsake cake top.

5. Diamond Wedding ($825): Same as Emerald, plus thirty-six professional photographs.

Celebrity Cruise Line

1. Celebrity Wedding in port in Ft. Lauderdale ($525) or Celebrity Wedding in port in New York ($650): Includes transportation, official civil ceremony on board ship, couple's flowers, champagne, small wedding cake, wedding certificate and one hour of photographer's services.

2. St. Thomas Shipboard Celebrity Wedding ($600): Includes transportation from ship to St. Thomas courthouse to be sworn in for marriage

license and return to ship for ceremony, minister to officiate ceremony, couple's flowers, champagne, small cake, wedding certificate and one hour of photographer's services.

3. St. Thomas Shoreside Celebrity Wedding ($900): Includes transportation from ship to St. Thomas courthouse to be sworn in for marriage license, transportation to wedding site at either Magen's Bay or Blackbeard's Castle, minister to officiate ceremony, couple's flowers, mini-reception, champagne and champagne flutes, small wedding cake and wedding certificate.

Royal Caribbean

1. Special Value Package ($215): Civil ceremony performed to a background of taped music.
2. Special Value Package ($445): Same as above, plus parchment certificate and professional photography with album and thirty photos.
3. Royal Wedding Package ($635): Includes transportation, couple's flowers, civil ceremony, background music, certificate, photography with album and thirty photos, small wedding cake and champagne.

As you can see, a cruise ship wedding package is very affordable, especially compared to a full-blown hometown wedding! Cruise ship honeymoon packages are quite affordable as well, especially when you consider that they are all-inclusive.

Contact Cruise Lines, Inc. for the current catalog of sailing dates and prices. To give you an idea of just how affordable these cruises can be, here are some of the advertised specials that happen to be available through Cruise Lines, Inc. as this book goes to print:

• Carnival's Sensation: Seven-day round-trip (inside cabin) from Miami to San Juan, St. Thomas and St. Maarten: From $525 per person, double occupancy.
• Royal Caribbean's Grandeur of the Seas: Seven-day round-trip (inside cabin) from Miami to Labadee, San Juan, St. Thomas,

CocoCay: From $749 per person, double occupancy.

- Celebrity Century: Seven-day round-trip (inside cabin) from Ft. Lauderdale to San Juan, St. Thomas, St. Maarten, Nassau: From $749 per person, double occupancy.

In most cases, low "air add-ons" also are available that provide extremely affordable air transportation from your city to point of embarkation, in addition to "honeymoon perks" aboard the ship, such as Honeymooner's Cocktail Party, Breakfast in Bed and Champagne and Fruit Basket in your cabin. Give Cruise Lines, Inc. a call and they'll tell you all about it. Of course, any prices listed above are current as this book goes to print and subject to change.

Combine one of the Cruise Ship Honeymoons with a Cruise Ship Wedding and you'll have a fantastic, worry-free destination wedding idea!

SUCCESS STORY # 7

Lynn and Andy Cornwell

Lynn and Andy Cornwell were married on March 19, 1997, beside the Governor's House on Seven Mile Beach in Grand Cayman as their Princess Cruise ship "parked" offshore. Their wedding was arranged by Karen Emery at A Wedding for You. Karen is a member of the Association of Bridal Consultants and is a destination wedding planner who specializes in cruise-related weddings.

Lynn wore a summery, silk floor-length wedding gown, and her best friend and "quite pregnant" matron of honor wore a stunning bright fuchsia dress. Andy and his best man, better half to the matron of honor, wore tuxes that were ordered ahead of time by the cruise line. Of course, the matron of honor and best man accompanied Andy and Lynn on their seven-day cruise and everything was planned ahead of time, with one interesting hitch—only one person back home in Minnesota knew about the wedding plans. What a juicy secret!

Let's flash back for a moment so you can see what led up to this deliciously devious elopement. Andy and Lynn met for the first time in 1982 while they were attending a vocational school together—she was taking accounting classes and he was studying to become a diesel mechanic. Because each of them had serious "significant others" in their lives at the time, they were only friends, although they enjoyed seeing each other every day in the lunchroom.

Fast forward to 1992! Ten years went by before they met again at a sports bar. Lynn was there with two girlfriends, and Andy had dropped by with his brothers and their wives after a hockey game. She recognized him right away but couldn't remember his name. She was dying to talk to him though so she "just happened to walk by his table" on the pretense of asking the bartender for change.

They spoke briefly. He asked her if she was married yet, and she said, "No, and you?" Well, it turns out he was still single, too!

When Lynn returned to her table one of her girlfriends insisted Lynn give Andy her name and phone number. Lynn refused until her girlfriend said, "If you don't do it, I *will*." So, to avoid being embarrassed by her friend, she bravely stopped by Andy's table and handed him her business card. Sure enough, he called her the next day—not just once, but three times.

After their first date to a professional basketball game, they went to the same sports bar, where they sat and talked for four hours. Their relationship grew from there, and they dated for five years before finally deciding to get married.

They might be single still, in fact, if Andy's uncle hadn't pushed for them to marry. Over the years he kept telling Lynn to "crowd him—crowd him." He wanted them to get married in the worst way! Finally, on one of their long drives to visit this uncle, Lynn asked Andy, "What will we say when he asks us when we're going to get married?"

This started a discussion about marriage, and they decided that if they ever *were* going to get married, "Wouldn't it be nice to marry while your uncle is still around to enjoy it?"

So, they started talking "wedding" with each other privately— who would be in their wedding party, where they would be married, and so forth. When they realized they really "just had to have" a wedding party that totaled thirty-six people, they backed down from the idea of a formal hometown wedding and began to talk about getting married secretly while on a cruise.

Meanwhile, they *still* weren't officially engaged until one evening when they went to dinner with their best friends at McCall's Steak House in downtown St. Paul. After they had ordered dessert, Lynn and Rachel, her eventual matron of honor, went to the ladies room together where Lynn asked Rachel to "please work on Andy about getting me an engagement ring." (By this time Andy and Lynn had been together for five years and had even bought a house together—you can see why an engagement ring seemed like a *real* good idea!)

The women returned to the table just in time for the waiter to serve their desserts. He served the men first, which Lynn thought was strange. Finally, the waiter brought her a very fancy plate that had a ring box in the center of it. Her engagement ring was accompanied by Andy's formal proposal and a champagne celebration.

Soon after they were officially engaged, the four of them concocted a plan whereby they would all take a cruise together and, during the cruise, Andy and Lynn would elope to Grand Cayman Island. And that brings us back to our wedding on the beach.

Andy and Lynn stood with their best friends and recited their vows during a touching, prayerful ceremony. Lynn said, "We felt like a prince and princess—it was just so wonderful!"

Karen Emery had everything there for them—a videographer and photographer, the women's bouquets and the men's boutonnieres, the minister, and a mini-reception that was set up right on the beach, including a delicious wedding cake. There was even a silver ice bucket mounted in the sand!

The day Lynn and Andy returned from their cruise, one of Lynn's friends (the only person who knew they were getting married in Grand Cayman) hosted a "They Took the Grand Plunge in Grand Cayman" party for the couple, which was followed a few weeks later by a formal dinner-dance reception hosted by Lynn and Andy and their parents. Their parents didn't know they were getting married during their trip until Lynn and Andy called to tell them right after the ceremony.

By the way, when I asked Lynn how much the wedding and minireception cost, she said the whole thing totaled less than $1,200. Imagine that! Now that's the way to get married! ♡

SANDALS RESORTS

Sandals Resorts, advertised as "The Caribbean's #1 Ultra All-Inclusive Luxury Resort for Couples Only," owns ten tropical hideaways on four islands: Jamaica, Antigua, St. Lucia and the Bahamas.

Sandals Resorts are popular honeymoon destinations because:
- They offer the ultimate in luxury and amenities.
- They ooze with "romance" and "sensuality."
- You're pampered day and night.
- Everything is included in one price, including tips.
- They offer fantastic entertainment, festivities and theme parties.
- All feature white sand beaches and clear, turquoise water.
- All offer beachfront/ocean-view rooms.
- The Jamaica resorts offer Stay at One, Play at All Six resorts.
- The St. Lucia resorts offer Stay at One, Play at Both.
- All resorts offer sauna, whirlpool and steambaths.
- Dozens of activities are available, depending on location, including water sports, pool, tennis, racquetball, golf, basketball, lawn chess, shuffleboard, horseshoes, croquet, dancing in a discotheque or nightclub and, of course, swimming in the pools or the ocean.

The resorts offer all-inclusive honeymoon packages for any size budget, from a three-night stay in a deluxe room at Sandals Montego Bay for about $670 per person, to a seven-night stay in a one-bedroom Sunset Ocean Suite with private swimming pool at Sandals St. Lucia for about $3,525 per person. A six-night stay in a fabulous room at most of their locations runs less than $3,000 total, which is pretty amazing when you consider everything that's included.

By the way, there are also various Delta Dream Vacations packages available for many Sandals Resorts, which include round-trip air transportation from Miami, but you will need to contact Delta's Vacation Center to inquire about their current offerings.

Sandals' WeddingMoon packages are very affordable wedding packages that start at about $750.

A typical WeddingMoon package includes:

- Services of a personal wedding coordinator
- Marriage certificate and ceremony officiant
- Wedding reception in a decorated location, three bottles of champagne and a Caribbean two-tiered wedding cake
- Flower bouquet and boutonniere
- 5" × 7" wedding photo and professional video
- "Honeymoon" candlelight dinner for the bride and groom
- Continental breakfast in bed the morning after the wedding

Sandals also offers a more complete wedding package called The Royal Wedding, which is available only at Sandals Royal Jamaican and Sandals Royal Bahamian, where you can be married in a horse-drawn winged carriage in a fairy-tale wedding. In fact, the entire wedding is designed to make you feel like genuine royalty by lavishing you with sumptuous extravagance in every detail.

Whether you choose one of their standard WeddingMoon packages, or you opt for the "royal treatment," you're assured a romantic, worry-free wedding that has been arranged by an experienced, professional wedding coordinator who leaves nothing to chance. In fact, every couple I've interviewed had nothing but praise for their Sandals Resort wedding.

PINEAPPLE BEACH CLUB ON LONG BAY, ST. JOHN'S, ANTIGUA

This is another great choice for couples looking for an affordable all-inclusive resort. Although this resort is not quite as elegant and pretentious as some, it's absolutely wonderful for the couple who's looking for a quiet, romantic spot to get married and spend their honeymoon.

Pineapple Beach Club sits on one of the best beaches in all of Antigua. White sand shimmers in the sun, and waters are sheltered by protective reefs—

perfect for every kind of water sport. Because this resort is located on twenty-five acres of secluded land, it is perfect for the honeymooning couple who wants to stroll down the beach undisturbed.

There are four tennis courts, all kinds of water sports and reef fishing, plus fishing excursions to surrounding islands. Plenty of other activities are available as well, including a romantic cruise to Bird Island, volleyball, nature trails and the Pirate's Den, an electronic casino.

Honeymoon rates range from about $320 to $460 per couple per night and are *all-inclusive*, which means that your meals, drinks, water sports, fitness center, tennis, entertainment, transfers, gratuities, service charges and government taxes are included in the package price. The only things that aren't included are radios, television sets and telephones in each room, although they are available in the main reception building. Of course, if you're planning on spending your honeymoon talking to your mother on the telephone or watching *Jeopardy* and *Wheel of Fortune*, this may not be the best choice for you anyway!

Pineapple Beach Club's basic wedding packages start at about $600 and include normal government fees, registrar costs, ceremony charges, decorated ceremony and reception sites, bride's bouquet and groom's boutonniere, wedding cake, a bottle of champagne and all taxes, service charges and gratuities. Not bad, huh? And here's an even better deal: If you stay in one of their upgraded rooms for at least thirteen nights, the wedding is free!

HALF MOON GOLF, TENNIS AND BEACH CLUB, MONTEGO BAY, JAMAICA

Set on four hundred manicured acres of beachfront property, this resort features clusters of villas and suites, many with private swimming pools. Not only is it one of my favorites, but it is also the favorite of celebrities from all over the world, including Sean Connery, the Beatles, Prince Charles and President George Bush. Why is this resort so appealing? For many reasons:

- Its mile-long white crescent beach
- The white plantation villas and beach houses that are tastefully placed along the palm-lined beach
- The gardens bulging with red and orange bougainvillea that glim-

mer against the stark white of the villas and wicker patio furnishings

- The Robert Trent Jones 72-hole championship golf course
- Fitness center, horseback riding, hiking trails
- Many freshwater swimming pools
- Water sports galore, including deep-sea fishing
- Three excellent restaurants and dancing to a live band or at the discotheque
- Beach parties, floor shows, native entertainment and drum bands

The Half Moon's special wedding package, priced under $700, includes marriage officer, witnesses, flowers, champagne, video, cake and photos and takes place in the Fairytale Gazebo which sits on a peninsula of land that juts out into the ocean. Truly magical! All-inclusive honeymoon stays start at about $450 per couple per night.

What a wonderful place to get married and spend your honeymoon!

SUPERCLUBS LIDO RESORTS: SANS SOUCI LIDO IN OCHO RIOS AND GRAND LIDO IN NEGRIL

These two SuperClubs "super-inclusive" resorts are considered by many to be two of the most lavish, luxurious and romantic in the Caribbean. However, they are not for the couple who wants to honeymoon on a budget—a seven-night stay at Sans Souci Lido, Ocho Rios, can run as high as $3,330 per person, double occupancy. Oh, well, it's only money!

You get what you pay for, though, because their "super-inclusive" prices include incredibly sensual and romantic ambience created by such things as:

- A lighted rock gazebo that hangs over the moonlit, iridescent blue-green ocean
- Many luxurious suites with king-size beds and in-room whirlpools
- Secluded hammocks and hidden grottos
- Irresistibly titillating night-blooming jasmine
- Breakfast in bed
- Candlelight dancing

And, best of all for those of you who are looking for a truly worry-free wedding, their weddings are not only complete with license, minister, flowers, champagne and a traditional Jamaican wedding cake, but they are *absolutely free*! You can be married in that rock gazebo I mentioned, or aboard a 147-foot yacht, in one of their lush gardens, on the beach or *any place* you would like!

So easy! So romantic!

SUPERCLUBS BREEZES: BREEZES RUNAWAY BAY IN JAMAICA, BREEZES MONTEGO BAY IN JAMAICA AND BREEZES BAHAMAS IN NASSAU

All three Breezes resorts are adults-only, all-inclusive resorts, and they all offer free weddings, similar to the weddings described above for the SuperClubs Lido resorts, with many romantic ceremony settings from which to choose, including an exquisite Wedding Gazebo at Breezes Runaway Bay.

All these Breezes resorts offer those wonderful amenities you come to expect from one of these all-inclusive honeymoon havens, including:

- All meals and tips
- Water sports
- Tennis, volleyball, etc.
- Fitness center
- Golf available at Breezes Runaway Bay
- Special activities, such as Toga Party, Pajama Party, Body Painting Contests, Talent Show, steel bands, glass-bottom boat rides, horse-and-buggy rides and more
- And, of course, they are all on white sand beaches

These resorts are considered affordable by Caribbean resort standards, with seven-night stays starting at about $1,100 per person, double occupancy.

A word about Caribbean marriage requirements: To marry anywhere in the Caribbean, you'll need these documents, plus others as required by each country:

- Certified copies of birth certificates
- Certified copies of divorce papers (if applicable)

- Certified copies of death certificate of deceased spouse (if applicable)

All "certified copies" must have original stamp or seal and signature, and all must be in English.

Additional requirements by country are as follows:

For Jamaica:
- Allow three working days for processing of marriage license and a minimum of twenty-four hours' residence in Jamaica.
- Bring passports and photo IDs.
- No blood test required.
- Call the Jamaica Tourist Board for more details at (800) 233-4582.

For the Bahamas:
- Both parties must appear in person at the registrar general's office in Nassau to file the application; you must both produce a photo ID issued by an office of the U. S. government and evidence of your arrival in the Bahamas (e.g., airline tickets).
- You must have a declaration certifying both are unmarried U.S. citizens, sworn before a U.S. consul at the American Embassy, Nassau, *or* a marriage license from the Commissioner's Office on other islands.
- The Bahamas Ministry of Tourism has recently relaxed the rules for residency to twenty-four hours: call (800) NUPTIAL for more information.
- No blood test required.

For United States Virgin Islands:
The four islands of the United States Virgin Islands—St. Thomas, St. John, St. Croix and Water Island—are all U. S. territories, so getting married there is similar to getting married at home. Here is what you will need:
- Get a marriage license application in advance by writing to the Territorial Court of your chosen island.
- Bring documentation of any previous marriages (a divorce decree or certificate of death of former spouse).

- A letter must accompany your Application for Marriage stating date of visit, length of stay and preference of date if having ceremony performed by a judge.
- There is an eight-day waiting period.
- No blood test required.
- Call the U.S.V.I. Department of Tourism for complete information at (800) 372-USVI.

For British Virgin Islands:
- There is a three-day waiting period.
- No blood test required.

For Aruba:
- Jewish—U.S. marriage certificate and verification of Judaism from home rabbi and petition to the Aruba Jewish community.
- Christian—U.S. marriage certificate.
- Roman Catholic—marriage permit from home priest, baptism certificate and official form stating that neither party was ever married in a church.
- There is no waiting period, and no blood test is required.

Resorts that offer weddings on their premises will help you with all these requirements, or you can call the Caribbean Tourism Organization at (212) 682-0435 or fax them at (212) 697-4258 for more information.

Other Destinations

If your honeymoon destination wasn't included on my list of favorites but you like the idea of being married at your honeymoon resort or hotel, call the concierge and ask if a wedding can be arranged by the resort's staff. If not, you may want to call a destination wedding planning specialist who arranges destination weddings at sites all over the world, including Canada and Europe. (I have made reference to several in the appendix, including members of the Association of Bridal Consultants who arrange weddings in Germany, France, Singapore, the Caribbean, Mexico and Hawaii.)

I don't think you can go wrong by choosing a destination wedding—it may be the perfect answer for you!

THINGS TO REMEMBER:

○ Get all legal marriage requirements *in writing* and in plenty of time to meet them: age and residency requirements, parental consent and birth certificate, passport, blood test reports, etc.

○ Double-bag your wedding gown and carry it on board the plane.

○ When purchasing a gown for a destination wedding, avoid fabrics that don't travel well, such as taffeta or linen.

○ To cut down on costs, schedule your destination wedding during the shoulder (the week or two on either side of the prime tourist season) or off season, and make your travel arrangements at least thirty days in advance.

○ The majority of destination weddings have no guests—the wedding coordinator provides witnesses for the ceremony.

○ Use only a credit card to make any deposits or payments for your destination wedding arrangements. This allows you a certain amount of federal consumer protection in case of disputes.

○ When booking your travel, try to find a travel agent who has actually *been* to the site and seen it firsthand.

○ When traveling outside the United States, the name on all documents and identification should be the same, including passport, airline tickets, driver's license and any other identification. Because it can take a month or more for the bride's passport to be reissued in her married name, she should plan on traveling under her maiden name.

○ READ THE FINE PRINT IN ALL CONTRACTS BEFORE SIGNING!

CHAPTER FOUR

The Informal Wedding

The idea of an informal or casual wedding is popular not only because it is so affordable, but also because it is so easy to plan.

The casual wedding is considered by many to be more relaxed, more fun, and *much* less stressful than a traditional wedding, and it is especially popular for a second marriage when the bride or groom has already done the "big wedding thing" and wants something less nerve-wracking and time-consuming this time.

What kind of weddings am I talking about? Actually, any wedding that breaks with tradition can be considered an informal wedding, but generally they fall into one of these three categories:

- The K.I.S.S. Wedding
- The Surprise or Combination Wedding
- The Novelty Wedding

A K.I.S.S. Wedding

K.I.S.S. means "Keep It Sweet and Simple." And what are the rules for one of these weddings? There aren't any! Isn't that beautiful?

Here are a few examples of a K.I.S.S. wedding.

BEACH PARTY WEDDING

Bring your best man and maid of honor along as witnesses and get married in a brief civil ceremony performed at the county courthouse by a judge or a justice of the peace. Then, to celebrate, get together with your friends for an afternoon at the beach. Any beach will do, whether at the ocean, beside a lake or on a riverbank.

While the hamburgers and hotdogs are cooking on the grill, your friends can play Frisbie or beach volleyball or, if you're on a lake, some may prefer to water-ski. Later, as the sun begins to set, gather around the campfire, pull out the iced champagne and receive your toasts of congratulations.

By the way, depending on where you live, you may be able to have a friend or family member legally deputized for the day, which means that this person could perform the marriage ceremony right there on the beach. This idea can work for other weddings described in this chapter as well. Contact your local county clerk's or county recorder's office to find out if it is possible to have someone deputized to legally officiate at your wedding.

Many ministers are also available to perform marriage ceremonies at informal weddings, which works out really well if you want to get married on a Saturday when most county offices are closed and it isn't possible to be married in a judge's chambers.

"DENIM REQUIRED" WEDDING

You've all heard of "tie required" or "jacket required." Well, this is a wedding where "denim is required." I heard about this idea when I was interviewing Sandy Ezrine of Weddings in Sedona who was featured in chapter one. She said that this idea is really catching on in Arizona and is especially popular for a wedding with a western theme. Everyone, including the bride and groom, wears denim in one form or another.

The wedding and/or the reception that follows is usually held in a rustic setting with an improvised dance floor where the guests can square dance, line dance or do the Macarena!

PARTICIPATION WEDDING

Here's another popular informal wedding idea contributed by Sandy. She said that sometimes a simple wedding ceremony is held at one of the small country churches in her area, followed by a fun "participation party," sometimes held in her three-acre backyard. Or, the officiant may marry the couple at the reception site itself.

In either case, the guests are told to bring along shorts, T-shirts and tennis shoes to change into for the "participation" games: horseshoes, volleyball, badminton, croquet, and so forth. As Sandy said, it's a "very loose, easy-going fun time—nothing fancy about it."

PATIO PARTY WEDDING

Whether it has a Polynesian theme with Tiki torches and flowered leis, an Italian theme with checkered tablecloths and "drippy" candles or absolutely no theme at all, what could be more relaxing and fun than a patio party where you can be surrounded by your closest friends and family members? It can be a potluck supper or just a few side dishes to go with the steaks sizzling on the grill—the important thing is to keep things simple. Of course, if there happens to be a pool handy, it might turn into a swim party as well.

THEME PARK WEDDING

Almost everyone lives within a fairly reasonable distance of some type of theme park. Get married in a civil ceremony right before you go, or if one of your friends has been deputized, bring him or her along and do what one couple did—get married on top of the Ferris wheel. Then, spend the rest of the day enjoying the park with your friends. Of course, when you're ready to make your escape, you can always leave everyone else there to party until closing time!

PICNIC IN THE PARK WEDDING

A picnic in the park is a lot like a patio party or a beach party, except that it takes place in a park. It can be any kind of park—it doesn't matter, just so it's beautiful and has plenty of space. For example, a lot of couples get married at Yosemite National Park in California where for a fee of only $25 the ceremony can be performed wherever they like.

Another popular spot is the Rose Garden at Golden Gate Park in San Francisco, which is available to residents and nonresidents alike for the bargain fee of only $125 for two hours, with the adjacent picnic area available for an additional $75 for all day. What a deal! And what a setting!

Another option is to have a "Good Ole Days Picnic" at your favorite park close to home, with sack races, three-legged races, an egg toss, Frisbie-throwing contest, Hoola Hoop contest or any other silly thing you can think to do. The object is to keep it light and fun and to enjoy your wedding day with your friends.

A HOUSEBOAT WEDDING

Rent a houseboat for the weekend, bring your friends and your officiant, and get married on board. Party until the sun goes down. Then, return to port, say goodbye to your guests and cast off once more to spend your honeymoon alone.

Another idea would be to get married on a ferryboat as it glides across San Francisco Bay or a paddleboat as it chugs down the Mississippi River.

♡   ♡   ♡

Do any of these ideas whet your appetite for a K.I.S.S. wedding? If so, you'll enjoy this Success Story about a couple who were married in a very simple ceremony after Sunday morning church.

S U C C E S S   S T O R Y   # 8

Scott and Bonnie

Scott and Bonnie were married in September 1996 in a simple but touching ceremony that took place on the patio of his parents' home in San Antonio, Texas. Not only was it the joining of two people who were very much in love, but also the healing of two grief-stricken hearts.

Bonnie's first marriage ended in divorce in 1992 when her husband informed her that he was leaving her to marry a woman who worked for him. At the time of the divorce, Bonnie was left with a son, eight, and a daughter, six.

Scott's wife had died of cancer in 1994, and he was left with three boys to raise who were nine, eleven and thirteen at the time. He wanted to "be there" for them, so he quit his job at a car dealership where he worked over seventy hours a week and studied to become a stockbroker. This meant fewer hours and the chance to work from home part of each day.

After becoming single parents, neither was the least bit interested in marrying again, and both Scott and Bonnie devoted all their spare time and energy to raising their children. Through the years they were involved in almost everything from Pop Warner football to Little League to soccer. Although they realized later that their paths must have crossed many times, they never met until March 1996 at a citywide soccer tournament their children were involved in.

Unlike so many couples who meet and whose love grows over time, their first meeting was an explosion of physical attraction and love at first sight. Bonnie was sitting in the stands with her daughter. She said it was a "beastly hot day" so she had brought along a cooler full of canned juices. Scott arrived a little late, sat down a few feet away from her and stripped off his shirt because of the heat. Bonnie, the brave divorcee who had sworn off men for the rest of her life, suddenly became flustered by the looks of him as he sat there bare-chested. Then, when he turned to her and she got a better look at the rest of him, she was a total "goner."

Scott said, "Hot day, isn't it?"

To which she stammered, "Uhhhhh, would you like some cold juice?"

He replied, "Don't mind if I do." And from that small beginning, one thing led to another. The next thing they knew they were talking away about their favorite subjects—their kids.

Now, to hear it from Scott, he had taken one look at her—sitting there in her short white shorts, long tanned legs and her "cute blond pony tail sticking out the back of her baseball cap"—and had the same reaction to her. This surprised him because he'd been around a lot of good-looking women since his wife died and had never had this happen before.

In the process of their conversation he found out that she worked at a bank just two blocks from his office, so he suggested that "maybe they could get together for lunch sometime." And they did—*many* times, in fact. Then they started getting together in the evenings and on weekends, including their children as often as they could.

By the middle of April they each knew in their hearts that they wanted to get married, but nothing had been said, of course, because it was so soon after they'd met. Scott had originally suggested they take it nice and slow and "see how it's going in a year or so." Well, that was a laugh, because by the end of the summer they not only *knew*, but were talking marriage.

On Labor Day weekend Scott took Bonnie to dinner at the River Grill. After dinner they walked for a while along the Riverwalk, and then he proposed to her during a romantic gondola ride down the San Antonio River. She accepted, of course, and they spent the rest of the weekend talking about wedding plans. They thought a Christmas wedding would be nice.

Well, a Christmas wedding *would* have been nice except for one thing: It would be way too tough to wait that long, especially since they both had strong religious convictions against sleeping together before marriage. Scott laughs when he tells it. "Here I was a leader of a group of high school boys in my church and I'd been telling them how important it was to stay celibate until they married, so I knew I'd better figure out a way to marry Bonnie *real* quick, or I'd end up the biggest hypocrite in the state of Texas." So, Scott made an "executive decision" to get married as soon as they could.

Because Bonnie's parents were serving as missionaries in Japan and wouldn't be able to fly home for a wedding anyway, Scott cooked up a plan with his parents to be married at their home ten days later. He asked a good friend, one of the pastors at his church, to "come over after church a week from Sunday and marry us."

Bonnie and her sister took an afternoon off to shop for Bonnie's dress, a soft peach tea-length chiffon, and a few things for the honeymoon, which would be spent at the Coronado Hotel in San Diego.

Fifteen people attended their wedding, including the minister and his wife. Scott's dad had spruced up the landscaping in the backyard and added several hanging baskets of bougainvillea to the patio. His mom put together a nice Sunday brunch, including a small wedding cake. Their five children, who were really excited about their parents getting married and "totally into the day," took turns with the camera and video-cam. The afternoon flew by, and by five o' clock Scott and Bonnie were off to the airport for their flight to San Diego.

Two weeks after the wedding, they were given two receptions, one hosted by the congregation of Scott's church and one by the employees at the bank where Bonnie worked. Then, because their wedding expenses had been minimal, they were able to afford a week with their kids at Disney World over Christmas vacation. Bonnie told me, "Our wedding day was so relaxed and so much fun—we have no regrets." ♡

A Surprise or Combination Wedding

Here's another popular new fad: get married as part of some other celebration. The wedding itself can be a surprise, or it may be announced informally ahead of time, either over the telephone or by word of mouth.

Now, when I say a "surprise wedding," I don't mean that it's a surprise to the bride and groom—only to those in attendance. After all, the couple needs their blood tests and a marriage license ahead of time.

The only time I know of when the bride or groom *was* surprised was a wedding I saw on television where the bride and her bridesmaids arrived unannounced at the warehouse where the groom worked. The groom seemed to be pretty sweaty and grubby and in absolute shock to see her standing there in her elegant, floor-length wedding gown. It didn't bother the bride a bit, however, and the wedding took place right there amidst the warehouse dust and clutter. Evidently they had been planning a traditional wedding, but the plans had gotten out of control and become so stressful that the bride decided to bring them to one giant, screeching halt by springing the wedding on him at work.

Everyone involved—except I'm not too sure about the groom—seemed to think it was an adorable idea, but I have to say it really wasn't one of my favorite weddings!

So, when I recommend a "surprise wedding," the bride and groom are *always* in on the plans!

The opportunities for combining a wedding with another event are almost limitless. They can involve any kind of party you can think of, any type of family get-together or any sport or hobby known to man.

PARTIES

Office Christmas Party

If you met at work and all your co-workers observed your romance with vicarious relish, and if you like your co-workers and you feel close to them, a surprise wedding may be a terrific idea for the annual Christmas party. Get the word out that this year's party will have a "special surprise," just to keep everyone in suspense!

Come as You Are Party

This is a party where people are called on the spot and told to drop everything and "come as you are." Depending on what everyone happens to be wearing at the time of the telephone call, this can turn out to be a pretty funny party. Of course, the best surprise of all is the fact that, not only have they "come as they are," but they have come to watch you get married. Talk about a "casual wedding"—this is it!

Valentine's Party

What could be more appropriate than a wedding during a Valentine's party? It's a day meant for lovers anyway, so why not top it off with the most romantic thing of all—a real, live wedding!

On New Year's Eve

This is a really popular night for a wedding. There's something wonderfully exciting about starting out the new year as husband and wife.

During an Engagement Party or Boy-Girl Shower

Who's usually invited to one of these parties? The friends or family members closest to the couple, of course. So, why not surprise the heck out of them by getting married during the party? Just think—the decorations couldn't be more fitting, the guests more appropriate or the plans less stressful! What a great idea!

SPORTS GET-TOGETHERS

If you're involved in any kind of sport at all, as an observer or a participant, it can be easy to incorporate a wedding into the day.

Golf

If you're a member of a group that golfs together regularly and your golfing buddies are your best friends, you may want to get married at the end of a tournament as one couple did. At the end of the weekend tournament when everyone was gathered around the eighteenth green for the awards ceremony, a white aisle runner was rolled out onto the green, taped music began to play "Here Comes the Bride" and the couple was married as their astonished friends watched in surprise.

Once everyone got the hang of what was going on, someone suggested they all hop into their golf carts and form a "wedding parade" around the course, which they did, ending up in the clubhouse to celebrate.

Other Sports

The same idea will work for any sport, whether you get married at center court after a tennis tournament, in the middle of your favorite lane at the bowling alley or at home base after the last game of the season for your slow-pitch softball league. Use your imagination, and remember—the idea is to keep it simple and get married without any hassle or stress.

Tailgate Party

For all of you avid, rabid, dyed-in-the-wool sports fans who have season tickets to every home game and wouldn't miss out even if you have a 101° temperature, this idea is for you. If you have been getting together with the same group of friends for years to watch your favorite team play—arriving hours before the game, of course; setting up in the parking lot with your grills, lawn chairs and ice chests; and enjoying every minute of the day, win or lose—why not spring your surprise before or after the "big game"?

You could be married during your tailgate party or after the game when you all get together at your favorite sports bar. It's something to think about!

CLUB FUNCTIONS
Dance Club

Any kind of dance, whether it's ballroom, square dancing or country-western, is already a festive affair, so what could be more fun than to initiate the evening with a wedding surprise?

Travel Club

Depending on what kind of travel is involved, you can be married while on a trip or during one of your monthly meetings. One couple, who were members of a travel club, pulled off a real coup, with not only a surprise wedding, but also a "secret meeting place." Only the bride and groom, the president of the club and the officiant were privy to the surprise, which began with everyone meeting at a designated spot in town where they were given a "treasure map."

By following clues on the map they located another map posted on a tree that gave them clues to find the next stop and next clue, and so forth. Of course, the object was to arrive at the "surprise destination" where the bride and groom were waiting, along with the officiant, iced champagne and, of course, a wedding cake.

This idea of a treasure map that leads club members to a "secret meeting place" works well with any kind of group, but it's especially appropriate for a travel club.

Singles Club

If you met each other through a singles club and you're close friends with the rest of the members, what could be more exciting than planning a surprise wedding for one of their meetings or parties (since it will most likely be the last one you attend)?

Gourmet Cooking Club

One couple I know met through a cooking club. When they became engaged, the suggestion was made for everyone to bring their favorite hors d'oeuvres to the next meeting, which would be a party in honor of the newly engaged couple. Then, when everyone arrived with their appetizers in hand, they realized that instead of an engagement celebration, they were there for a wedding. Nice surprise!

The bride and groom provided the wedding cake and champagne.

Toastmasters Club

This same idea could work just as well at a meeting of Toastmasters, which is an organization for people who want to learn how to deliver speeches and toasts. The twist is that everyone is to come to the next meeting prepared to deliver an original wedding toast from memory. When they arrive, of course, their toasts become the real thing.

Photography Club
The members of the club are told to come to the next meeting prepared to do a "surprise photo shoot." When they arrive they realize that their subjects for the shoot are the bride and groom.

Little Theater Group
A little theater group held a surprise wedding between two cast members on stage as a "curtain call" to their final performance of *Annie Get Your Gun*. Cute idea!

As you can see, a wedding can take place during any kind of club meeting, whether it is a surprise or not. The possibilities are limitless.

FAMILY GATHERINGS
If you're close to your family and nothing could be more meaningful than getting married during one of their gatherings, this may be a great idea for you. However, if you don't get along with certain family members, or if there is any kind of friction between them that would make for a sticky situation if you sprung a wedding on them unexpectedly, this is probably a bad idea.

If you do decide this may work for you, it's almost always best to plan it as a surprise, otherwise it becomes "A WEDDING," and everyone tries to make a big deal out of it, which is exactly what you were trying to avoid in the first place!

Here are a few possibilities.

During a Family Reunion
A family reunion usually brings relatives together from all over the state or the country, which presents the perfect opportunity to get married with all your loved ones present.

On Christmas Eve or Christmas Day

Unlike a family reunion that many distant relatives may attend, Christmas is usually a time when the immediate family gets together, which may be what you prefer anyway. The trick here is finding an officiant who is willing to give up his or her holiday to perform the marriage ceremony. This is a case where a deputized friend may be the answer.

During Parents' or Grandparents' Anniversary Party

Getting married near the end of one of these celebrations can be a great idea or not, depending on the situation. If your wedding surprise would make your parents or grandparents *so* happy that it would top off the occasion to perfection, then it may be a good idea. However, if your little surprise would take away from their special day, it would not. You know your parents and grandparents very well, and you know how they feel about your upcoming marriage, so use your best judgment.

During a Fourth of July Picnic

A lot of families get together for an all-day Fourth of July celebration, topped off with a fireworks display after dark. This could be the perfect occasion for your surprise wedding. Be sure that lighted sparklers are added to your wedding cake!

On Thanksgiving Day

Depending on the family, who's invited and how well they get along with each other, Thanksgiving can be a wonderful "surprise wedding day." Again, the problem may be finding an officiant who will marry you on a holiday, but if you can work that out and you are very close to your family, this may be a good idea for you. One advantage of this plan is that for the busy student or for anyone who can't take time off work, a Thanksgiving Day wedding provides the couple with a long weekend honeymoon.

Here is a Success Story of a couple who pulled this off perfectly. By the way, the reason why they didn't let their siblings in on the secret was because they knew their brothers and sisters very well and were *sure* they would be so excited that the word would leak out. It was really important to them that they catch everyone off guard, and they did, as you will see.

Shari and Keith Thompson

Shari and Keith were married on Thanksgiving Day at a surprise wedding at her parents' home. The only people who knew about the plans ahead of time were their parents and the judge who married them.

Keith had proposed to Shari on her birthday the previous July, and the plan had been to marry after they both graduated from Colorado State University the following summer. There was one major problem, however: They were already in debt with their school loans and couldn't figure out how they would save enough for a big wedding unless they put it off at least another year after graduation, which they felt was too long to wait.

So, with the help and encouragement of Shari's parents, they planned a surprise wedding for Thanksgiving Day. When Shari's relatives arrived, they were surprised to find a larger crowd than usual, including Keith's parents, brother and two sisters.

Dinner wasn't planned until two o'clock so everyone was sitting around munching on appetizers and watching football on TV when there was a knock at the front door and they were joined by the next door neighbors, Jim and Virginia. Everyone thought they had just been invited over for dinner; no one suspected that Jim was there to perform a marriage ceremony.

At one o'clock Shari's dad turned off the television and announced, "You've probably noticed that we're a little larger crowd than usual this year, and the reason is that we wanted you all to be here to share in a special surprise.

"Jim?"

Jim walked over to the fireplace and stood facing the guests. Then Shari whispered to her sister who, wide-eyed with surprise, stood and followed Shari. Keith beckoned to his brother, who was equally shocked, and the four of them stood together as Jim conducted the brief ceremony. Jim and Shari had written and memorized their vows and as they recited them to each other, there wasn't a dry eye in the room.

As you can imagine, the guests were in shock. They absolutely couldn't believe it! Everyone was talking at once, congratulating them, wanting to know how long this had been planned and how they'd managed to keep it such a secret.

The Thanksgiving dinner doubled as their wedding celebration, topped off by a small two-tiered wedding cake that had been hidden out of sight in Jim and Virginia's kitchen until after the ceremony. After Shari and Keith had cut the cake, Shari's uncle came up with a surprise of his own. He discreetly collected a joint wedding gift of checks and cash that totaled over $2,000, which he presented to them as they were about to leave for their Thanksgiving weekend honeymoon in Vail. Needless to say, they were really touched by this, and it enabled them to have a much nicer honeymoon than they had planned.

As this book goes to print, Shari and Keith have been married for three years and they look back on their wedding day with great fondness. Keith said, "It was perfect—we were surrounded by our families, and everyone's still talking about it. It was a great day!" ♡

A Novelty Wedding

A Novelty Wedding takes place at some truly bizarre and unusual spot—any clever setting will do, actually. Also, this type of wedding invariably draws a lot of media coverage. Here are some examples.

AT THE TOP OF THE SPACE NEEDLE

Several couples are married each year at the top of the Space Needle in Seattle. I've been up there recently and it seemed awfully windy, but it is definitely a popular spot to tie the knot.

ON TOP OF A BILLIARDS TABLE

Speaking of media coverage, I saw newspaper photos of a wedding that took place on top of the billiards table at the sports bar where the couple met. The entire wedding party managed to climb up there and it looked pretty crowded to me! Definitely qualifies as a Novelty Wedding in my book!

IN A '56 CHEVY CONVERTIBLE

Another couple was married while sitting in their decorated Chevy convertible during a Classic Car Show. Her maid of honor and his best man sat in the backseat and after the ceremony they led a parade of honking cars down Main Street.

AT A HOCKEY GAME

A wedding took place recently at center rink before a professional hockey game. Everyone wore skates, including the officiant. After the ceremony, the bride and groom skated under an arch created by the hockey players' crossed hockey sticks. It was a clever idea!

SKYDIVING

Many of you may have seen the skydiving wedding on television. It was on *Weddings of a Lifetime* and was preceded by the couple's love story—how they were both members of the skydiving club, became close friends, then fell in love, became engaged and eventually decided to have a skydiving wedding. The entire wedding party jumped out of the plane together, which was pretty amazing!

AT THE TOP OF A SKI LIFT

Getting married at the top of a ski lift has become such a popular idea that it has almost become commonplace. I have close personal friends who met while skiing, fell in love and decided to get married at the top of their favorite lift. If you and your friends are really into downhill skiing, this may be an interesting option.

OVER THE INTERNET

This is the very latest—getting married over the Internet. Scott Grusky, who tied the "virtual knot" when he married his bride over the Internet in June 1995, has created a Website: http://www.loop.com/~cyberlove that offers advice for other couples who are longing to log in when they get hitched.

Scott, who met his bride, Sandra, in an Internet chat room, said, "For us it was symbolic. It completed the circle."

As this book goes to print, Scott is in contact with sixty-seven couples who have either married over the Internet or are in the process of planning an Internet wedding.

Here is the story of Lisa and Andy Hunt who were married in November of 1996 over the World Wide Web.

SUCCESS STORY # 10

Lisa and Andy Hunt

Lisa Grosso, 40, from West Palm Beach, Florida, and Andrew Hunt, 33, from Wellington, Somerset, England, were married on November 1, 1996, in a cyber-marriage ceremony.

According to the couple's web page, Andy, code named "Cloud Nine," and Lisa, known as "Starr," met on Internet Relay Chat (IRC) in May 1996. Andy said that two people can get to know each other very quickly over a chat line and can really delve deeply into each other's feelings. He also said that although some people lie over a chat line, he and Lisa were honest with each other from the start, revealing everything, "warts and all."

After exchanging computerized photos of each other and "chatting" steadily for one week, Andy invited Lisa to come visit him, which she did. Andy said, "We spent a wonderful week together."

On July 27 Lisa flew over to visit him again, and Andy proposed to her. Their engagement was announced on their homepage on the Internet. Two days later they e-mailed wedding invitations to their Internet friends around the world, and a "virtual guest book" was set up on their web page to accept congratulations.

Their ceremonies were held at Taunton Cyber, a cyber café in the heart of Taunton, Somerset, England. Lisa wore an elegant white Cinderella-style wedding gown and veil, and Andy wore a dark suit. Andy's son held the rings, and the wedding was witnessed in person by close members of their families and a few Internet Relay Chat friends who came for the day. Their main congregation, of course, were the people around the world who were present via their Internet connections.

First, the couple's marriage was blessed over the Internet Relay Chat by Rev. Peter Murphy from his parish in Lyndhurst in New Forest, England. Then the couple was married online by a minister who conducted the service from his computer in Seattle, Washington. Following the two services, messages of congratulations came flooding in from people all around the world.

Finally, after signing off and celebrating with their family and friends, they flew to Florida for their honeymoon.

If the idea of an Internet wedding sounds good to you, you might want to check out Scott Grusky's website, mentioned earlier, which offers helpful advice on creating your own personal Internet wedding. ♡

I think you'll agree that a casual wedding has a lot going for it—low on stress and high on fun! If you're looking for a way to bypass the hassles, one of these weddings may be for you.

THINGS TO REMEMBER:

○ If you decide to have an informal wedding, don't let anyone pressure you into changing your mind. This is *your* wedding—*not* your Aunt Tilda's.

○ As you plan your wedding, remember that a smile is like a can of silicone spray—it helps everything run more smoothly. Don't lose your sense of humor!

○ There are no rules when planning an informal wedding—anything goes. In fact, make up the rules as you go along!

CHAPTER FIVE

The Do-It-Yourself Worry-Free Wedding

If none of my worry-free wedding ideas appeal to you so far, and you still have your heart set on a big, traditional wedding, here are your two options:

- Plan it yourself with as little stress as possible
- Hire a professional bridal consultant to plan it for you

We'll talk about hiring a professional in the next chapter, but for those of you "crafty," creative people who are determined to have hands-on control of your wedding, but with as little stress as possible, this chapter is for you.

I'm going to take you through the planning process, from setting up your budget, to hiring your vendors, to the wedding day itself, always with one goal in mind—to keep it as stress-free as possible.

The Three Imperatives

Before you read any further, let's see if you are willing to abide by these three imperatives. If you're not, a do-it-yourself worry-free wedding is probably not possible for you.

- You must be willing to stay organized.
- You must be willing to delegate.
- You must be willing to accept the least stressful options.

To stay organized, you will need to set up a do-it-yourself planning notebook or purchase one of the handy planners on the market, such as my *Big Wedding on a Small Budget Planner and Organizer*. And you'll have to *use* it—every day!

In order to delegate, you will need to be willing to give up control of certain projects. For example, if a friend offers to help out by tying all your pew bows, be willing to let her give it a try, even though you know in your heart that you can tie the best pew bows in town! And if your friend's efforts leave something to be desired and the pew bows need to be "doctored up" a little to pass inspection, so what? At least you were able to cross "pew bows" off your to-do list.

Finally, when I talk about "accepting the least stressful options," I mean that you will need to keep the planning as uncomplicated as possible. For example, when choosing a florist, it is much less stressful to go with one of the standard wedding packages, as opposed to a special order that requires unusual bouquets or arrangements composed of out-of-season flowers. You'd be surprised at the number of brides who arrive at their florists with a folder bulging full of photographs, ribbon samples and fabric swatches, along with requests for such things as fresh imported hothouse tulips for their November wedding!

Now, if you're one of those brides who will *insist* on having tulips in November, you may want to skip this chapter altogether, because you don't know what stress is until you discover the day before the wedding that the tulips didn't arrive in time!

If you're still with me, and you agree to these three imperatives, let's get started with some good, sensible worry-free advice.

Worry-Free Budget
STEP #1

Have a frank discussion with everyone who will be helping out with the cost of the wedding, so you'll know exactly how much money you'll have to spend. Although over 70 percent of all wedding expenses these days are paid by the bride and groom themselves, here is a list of who *traditionally* pays for what:

The bride and her family
- The bride's attire and trousseau
- Rental of ceremony and reception sites
- Flowers (except those purchased by groom)
- Photography and videography
- Music
- All reception expenses, including food, beverages and wedding cake
- All other expenses not paid by others

The groom and his family
- Groom's attire
- Rehearsal dinner
- Boutonnieres for the men, bride's bouquet, bride's going-away corsage, and mothers' and grandmothers' corsages
- Marriage license
- Officiant's fee

The bride's attendants
- Their attire
- Their transportation to and from the wedding
- Bridesmaids' luncheon for the bride, unless hosted by the bride
- A gift for the bride and a wedding gift for the couple

The groom's attendants
- Their attire
- Their transportation to and from the wedding
- Bachelors' dinner/party, if not hosted by the groom
- A gift for the groom and a wedding gift for the couple

Parents of junior attendants
- Junior attendants' attire

To keep the finances as stress-free as possible, it is important for everyone's wedding expenses to be clearly understood from the start.

STEP #2

The next step is to write down each expense and who is expected to pay for it. This can be done by entering the information in a purchased planner or by using the Budget Planner form shown on the following pages. You may want to enlarge it on a copy machine and insert it in a three-ring notebook.

On my Budget Planner, I have indicated typical percentages allotted for each expense. These percentages are *only* guidelines, however, and your budget breakdown may be entirely different.

If you've never planned a wedding before, you may not realize why it is so important to set up your budget in advance. It has nothing to do with "planning a wedding on a budget"—whether your wedding budget is $5,000 or $50,000 isn't the point. The point is that *nothing* registers higher on the "stress meter" than misunderstandings over wedding expenses. So, once you've established your budget, you've taken a giant step toward eliminating problems later on.

Worry-Free To-Do List

Once the budget is established, the next step is to plan your to-do list. The longer you have to plan, of course, the less stressful it will be, because there won't be so many things to do each month. For the sake of a worry-free wedding, I hope you have at least a year to plan, but in any case, here are some guidelines to follow. You may want to copy this to-do list and place it in your notebook, along with specific dates for each thing to be done prior to your "big day."

As Soon As Possible

- Arrange a meeting between bride's and groom's parents.
- Establish your budget.
- Set date and time of wedding.
- Reserve ceremony and reception sites.
- Select officiant.
- Select members of wedding party.
- Choose a theme and color scheme.
- Select a photographer and schedule engagement portrait.
- Start compiling guest list.
- Begin planning the reception, including the menu.
- Purchase wedding attire for bride, mothers and attendants.

Six Months Before the Wedding

- Order invitations, thank-you notes, napkins, etc.
- Select a florist.
- Select ceremony and reception musicians.

Budget Planner

Typical % of Budget		Name of Vendor	Amount	Who Will Pay
Bride's Attire	10%			
Groom's Attire	1%			
Bridesmaids' Attire	5%			
Groomsmen's Attire	3%			
Jr. Attendants' Attire	1%			
Ceremony Site	4%			
Reception Site	8%			
Caterer	11%			
Wedding Cake	2.5%			
Flowers	4%			
Music	10%			
Decorations	5%			
Photography	5.5%			
Videography	2%			
Rental Items	2.5%			
Personal Services (Hair, makeup, manicures)	3.5%			
Favors	1%			
Wedding Stationery and Programs	4%			
Transportation	2%			
Other	15%			
Total:	100%	Total: $		

Four Months Before the Wedding

- Finalize plans for reception food, beverages and cake.
- Finalize plans for ceremony and reception decorations.
- Select a videographer.
- Make or purchase favors, pew bows and other decorations.
- Arrange for makeup artist, hair stylist, manicurist, parking attendant, nursery workers and security personnel.
- Arrange for a wedding day coordinator.
- Arrange for helpers to attend the guest book and gift tables, serve as host or hostess, follow up on plans that have been made, transport wedding gifts from reception site to your home, return tuxedos to rental shop, return any other rental items and generally be there for the bride and her family to help absorb the stress of the planning.
- Make arrangements for transportation and guest accommodations.

Three Months Before the Wedding

- Make appointment for a physical exam.
- Plan ceremony details.
- Reserve the men's attire.
- Address the invitations.
- Establish gift registries.
- Make arrangements for all items that will need to be borrowed, rented or purchased.

Two Months Before the Wedding

- Have a meeting with all your helpers.
- Plan reception details, including seating charts, dance order, order of receiving line, order and timing of events.

Six Weeks Before the Wedding

- Mail the invitations.
- Get blood tests.

One Month Before the Wedding

- Apply for marriage license.
- Plan bridesmaids' luncheon.
- Write thank-you notes.
- Have final fitting for wedding gown.
- Verify RSVPs and call caterer with head count.
- Have a personal meeting with every vendor to make sure you're on the "same page."

Three Weeks Before the Wedding

- Arrange for all the men to be measured for their tuxedos.
- Pack for the honeymoon.

Two Weeks Before the Wedding

- Practice your wedding day makeup and hair style, with veil.
- Write and memorize your wedding vows, if applicable.

One Week Before the Wedding

- Make up a time schedule and mail to everyone involved in the wedding.
- Speak *personally* with each and every vendor and helper, confirming each one's responsibilities.

Day Before the Wedding

- Finish packing for the honeymoon.
- Rehearse your vows.
- Eat well; sleep well; take a hot, relaxing bath!

On Your Wedding Day

- Eat a good breakfast, and take it easy on the coffee!
- Allow plenty of time to have your hair styled, nails manicured and makeup applied so you can begin to dress two hours before the ceremony.
- Arrive at ceremony site in time for pre-wedding photos.

- Remember Murphy's Law and allow a little extra time in case of a broken fingernail, a misplaced earring or a traffic jam.
- Breathe!

Worry-Free Planning
WORRY-FREE THEMES

Once you've set up your budget and your to-do list, you're ready to begin the planning itself. The first step is to choose a theme. Your theme will determine a lot of things, including what type of ceremony and reception site you will want, what type of flowers, music and decorations you will have and, of course, what type of wedding attire will be worn by the wedding party. So, before you run out and place a deposit on a reception site or start trying on wedding gowns, decide on a theme.

In my books *Big Wedding on a Small Budget* and *Beautiful Wedding Decorations and Gifts on a Small Budget*, I talk about dozens of themes, but for our purposes here, I'll mention those that are the least likely to cause you stress.

A Garden Theme
- For an outdoor wedding in a garden, minimal decorations are required. You may want to rent white wood folding chairs and a white wedding arch.
- For an indoor wedding, you can decorate with a white arch, arbors, white picket fences, wrought iron benches, birdbaths, potted plants, shrubs and flowers, silk ficus trees and trailing ivy.

A Hawaiian Wedding
- For an outdoor wedding in a garden or around a pool, you're already halfway there. Float rafts of flowers in the pool and add Tiki torches, crepe paper flowers, colorful silk or fresh flower leis and conch shells. Purchase a bolt of Hawaiian fabric to drape around for color.
- For an indoor wedding, you can use everything but the Tiki torches, and, of course, there won't be a swimming pool. However, you may be able to borrow or rent a couple of portable, plug-in waterfalls. Or fill several small children's swimming pools with water and gold fish, and camouflage them with tropical plants and flowers.

Country-Western Theme

• Here's a theme that's popular and easy to put together. Whether in-doors or outdoors, you can decorate with bales of hay, saddles, lariats, cowboy hats, branding irons, red bandanas and checkered tablecloths. You may also want to refer to the Teton Mountain wedding described in chapter two.

Romantic Candlelight Theme

• This idea is very easy to put together, but it only works for an evening wedding. Incorporate as many candles as you can afford. Place them absolutely everywhere: in candelabra, along the altar railings, on windowsills, on tall candlesticks at the end of each pew, on the piano and organ, and in sconces mounted on pillars.

Strings of tiny white Christmas lights add to the effect as well, especially when added to greenery or used to outline doorways or window frames. Your attendants can carry lighted candles embedded in a floral oasis filled with fresh flowers. Give decorated candles to each guest to be lighted at the end of the reception, creating a glowing walkway as you and your husband make your getaway.

Other Worry-Free Theme Possibilities

• Depending on the time of year or your ethnic background, a holiday or ethnic theme may also be easy to put together. Take advantage of existing decorations that may already be in place at your ceremony or reception site.

WORRY-FREE SUPPLIERS
Step #1

The first step is to do some detective work and come up with suppliers who are reputable, dependable and competent. By suppliers, I mean those amateurs or professionals who will be supplying you with goods and services. If you already know who you would like to have photograph your wedding or cater your recep-tion because you're familiar with their reputations, you're a leg up on your plan-ning. If not, you can locate reputable suppliers in several ways.

• Ask recent brides for referrals.
• Ask any professional vendor you know and trust to refer you to other

vendors. For example, if you've settled on your photographer because you've seen his work and you're familiar with his excellent reputation, call him and ask his advice. He attends a lot of weddings and knows which videographers, florists, DJs, dance bands or catering services are best. Likewise, a florist may be able to refer you to a reputable photographer, and so forth.

• Attend a bridal show where you can visit with many vendors and collect their brochures for future comparison.

• Once you have begun to narrow your list of vendors, call the Better Business Bureau to ask if complaints have been filed against any of them.

• Call the vendors on your list to schedule three personal appointments with each type of vendor, for example, three caterers, three florists and three photographers. It usually works best, by the way, to schedule all the florists for one day, all photographers for another, and so forth. This way you won't be mixing apples with oranges, and it will be easier to keep the comparisons fresh in your mind.

Remember what I said about "delegating," and don't be afraid to solicit help with this first step. Your fiancé, as well as your friends and family members, can help you assemble your "short list" of possibilities.

Step #2

Keep your appointments, preferably no more than three each day, and look for a vendor with these qualities:

• Someone who is a nice person and who seems genuinely interested in you and your wedding plans.

• Someone who is calm and soft-spoken and who takes all the time necessary to explain each option. If the person continually interrupts your meeting by taking telephone calls or by leaving the room to handle other crises that seem to be developing on the spot, this may not be the vendor for you. You don't want to hire a vendor who seems stressed, because stress is "catching," and your goal is to keep things as stress-free as possible. You don't want someone like this involved in your wedding plans, and you certainly don't want to "catch" a case of stress between now and the wedding!

• Someone whose plans or ideas you like—that will work best for your wedding or reception. (See my "Worry-Free Hints and Questions to Ask," below.)

Step #3

• Decide on one supplier for each of your wedding needs.

• Ask the questions suggested below, then negotiate the terms and sign the contracts.

• Delegate the duty of staying in touch with these suppliers on a regular basis. (One of your friends may agree to call or drop by the florist from time to time; another can maintain contact with the caterer; perhaps your fiancé can stay in touch with the reception musicians, etc.)

WORRY-FREE HINTS AND QUESTIONS TO ASK
Ceremony Site: Worry-Free Hints

• Try to find a site that has no other events scheduled for the wedding day or the day before the wedding. This will prevent your being forced to cut the wedding rehearsal short or feeling hurried as you decorate or place the floral arrangements.

• Try to find a site that has as few restrictions as possible (see "Questions to Ask," next page).

• Try to find a site that also has reception facilities available or is close to your reception site.

• Book your site as soon as you've set your wedding date because the site may not be available if you procrastinate.

• Have a designated friend or family member (remember what we said about "being willing to delegate?") accompany you to your first meeting at the ceremony site, not only to meet the staff personally, but to be aware of what was discussed and agreed upon during the meeting. This person will then become a liaison between you and the contact person at the site, staying in touch and following up on the arrangements, right up to the wedding day itself.

Ceremony Site: Questions to Ask

- Name, location, telephone number and contact person for site?
- Name of officiant, if applicable?
- What fees are involved? (rental fee, custodial, lighting, sound, church's wedding coordinator)
- What equipment does the site have available? (kneeling bench, sconces, candelabra, aisle runner, pew hangers, arches, floral baskets, other)
- What equipment will you need to provide?
- What services are available? (organist, altar boys, choir, prerecorded music, other)
- Are there any restrictions? (No smoking? No rice? No cameras during ceremony? No videography during ceremony? No aisle runner or elaborate decorations allowed? Will you be allowed to write your own vows? Are the guests allowed to applaud before the recessional?)
- Are dressing rooms available?
- Is there adequate parking?
- Will there be any other events taking place that day?
- Will there be existing decor?
- Can the site be available the day before the wedding for rehearsal and decorating?
- What is the total cost for the site?

Reception Site: Worry-Free Hints

- Try to find a site that has no other events scheduled for the wedding day, which will allow plenty of time for it to be decorated and for the caterer and musicians to get set up.
- Try to find a site that has as few restrictions as possible (see "Questions to Ask," next page).
- Try to find a site that will also serve as your ceremony site or is fairly close to your ceremony site.
- Try to find a site that provides its own catering services, wedding cakes, and service personnel, including wait staff, bartender, cake cutters, security, parking valet, coatroom attendant and cleanup crew. (If the site provides its

own catering, see the hints and questions listed below under "Reception Food.")

• Book your site as soon as you've set your wedding date because the site may not be available if you procrastinate.

• Bring your designated helper with you to your first meeting at the reception site, because this person will be the one who will be following up with the personnel at the site between now and the wedding day.

Reception Site: Questions to Ask

• Name, location, telephone number and contact person for site?
• Site rental fee?
• Other fees?
• What equipment is available?
• What equipment will you need to provide?
• What services are included?
• Restrictions? (No smoking? No rice? No alcoholic beverages? Musical restrictions? Will you be allowed to furnish your own food, drink, wedding cake, cake cutters, servers, etc., if applicable?)
• How many hours will the site be available?
• Will there be existing decor?
• Are dressing rooms available?
• Is there adequate parking?
• Will there be any other events taking place that day?
• What is the total cost for the site?

Reception Food and Drink: Worry-Free Hints

• Try to find a full-service professional caterer who will not only provide and serve the food, drink and wedding cake, but who will provide all the service personnel, including wait staff, bartender and cleanup crew, and who will decorate the tables with linen cloths and table skirting.

• Select one of the caterer's standard wedding packages, which means there will be no special orders for ingredients that may not be available at the last minute for some reason or another (remember Murphy's Law), or that may require the caterer to prepare something he or she may not have prepared before.

• Bring your designated helper along with you the first time you meet with your caterer, not only to meet the caterer personally, but to know what was discussed and agreed upon during the meeting. This person will then become your liaison with your caterer, staying in touch with him or her and following up on the details, right up to the wedding day itself.

Reception Food and Drink: Questions to Ask

- Name, address, telephone number and name of contact person?
- What equipment is available?
- What does the food plan cost, and what does it include?
- What services are included? (bartender, food servers, cake cutter, cleanup, etc.)
- Are there any hidden charges, such as "corking fees," cake cutting fees, additional bar charges if the guests drink more than expected or hourly fees for overtime pay if the reception runs longer than expected?

Wedding Cake: Worry-Free Hints

- Order your cake through your caterer or through the catering services at your reception site. This will prevent any problems with transporting the cake to your reception site, such as the driver getting into a traffic accident on the way or dropping one of the layers as he assembles the cake, etc.
- Order a cake that has a buttercream frosting, and don't allow whipped cream to be used anywhere on or in the cake. Not only can it spoil easily, but using whipped cream between the layers is asking for disaster on a hot day!
- Don't try to get too fancy with the cake, such as asking for it to be tied in a fabric ribbon. Unless this is something the pastry chef has done before, you may be disappointed to find that the ribbon has soaked through with frosting or has slipped off the top layer, etc. Keep it simple. You can always "personalize" it with a cake top that expresses your personality or complements your theme.
- Don't order your cake from a supermarket bakery or from a private party. These can be wonderful alternatives if you're trying to save money, but they do present a certain amount of risk. For a worry-free wedding day, you need to order your cake from a reputable bakery or through your reception site or catering service, as mentioned above.

Wedding Cake: Questions to Ask

- Name, address, telephone number and name of contact person?
- What is the cost of the cake?
- Is delivery included?
- When will the cake be delivered to the reception site?
- What style of cake will it be, and how many servings will be provided?
- Will it be fresh baked or frozen?
- What rental items will be involved (columns, stands, fountains, etc.), and what are their costs?
- Are there any restrictions (must be kept frozen or refrigerated until last minute, cannot be delivered on a Sunday, other)?
- What are the source and cost of the cake top?
- What is the total cost?

Bride's Attire: Worry-Free Hints

- Purchase your wedding gown, headpiece and accessories as soon as you can after you've become engaged.
- Don't put off purchasing your dress until you lose weight—purchase a gown *now* that fits you *now*! If you lose weight, that's wonderful. All you will need to do is have the gown altered to fit you. I've known so many brides who purchased a gown in a smaller size because they were *absolutely sure* they would lose weight before the wedding. Of course, if they don't, which often happens, the bride rushes around to purchase a gown that fits her, or goes on a crash diet, jeopardizing her health and emotional stability. Talk about stress!
- Don't order a gown to be delivered six months from now. What if the bridal salon goes out of business? What if the manufacturer goes out of business? What if the order is misplaced or mishandled? What if the gown doesn't arrive on time? What if it arrives, but it is the wrong gown or the wrong size? Purchase a gown off the rack if at all possible. That way it will be hanging in your closet and there will be no last-minute crises. If you can't find one that fits you off the rack, purchase one a size larger and have it altered to fit, or order through Penney's catalog where gowns run from size 4 to size 26W. Or, fly to Kleinfeld's in Brooklyn or travel to a factory outlet store, such as Gunne

Sax in San Francisco. Anything to avoid special-ordering a gown that may or may not arrive as promised!

• Once you have your gown, purchase the rest of your accessories as soon as you can. As your wedding day approaches, you don't want to be running around shopping for shoes or a petticoat!

Bride's Attire: Questions to Ask

• Is the style and length of the gown suitable for the theme I have chosen?

• Will it be appropriate for the ceremony and reception settings?

• Should I order a detachable train so I can enjoy myself during the reception?

• Will alterations be required? If so, who will make them?

• What is the cost of alterations?

• Is the veil or headpiece included?

• What is the cost of bridal accessories? (shoes, undergarments, gloves, garters, detachable train, etc.)

• What is the total cost?

Bridal Attendants' Attire: Worry-Free Hints

• Follow the same advice given to the bride above.

• Don't get hung up on purchasing the attendants' attire through a bridal salon. Try the "After Five" or "Finer Dress" departments of your local Macy's, Bloomingdale's, Nordstrom's, or other fine department store. There's nothing quite as much fun as finding just the right dress, one in each size required.

• The tendency when all of you shop together for the attendants' dresses is for everyone to start arguing over which dress looks best, so *you* need to take charge and decide which gown you prefer. Otherwise you'll spend five Saturdays shopping, instead of only one!

• Designate your honor attendant to be the one in charge of seeing to it that all alterations are made, all accessories are purchased and that all gowns have been steam-pressed in time for the big day.

Bridal Attendant's Attire: Questions to Ask

• Is the style and length of the gown suitable for the theme I have chosen?

• Will it be appropriate for the ceremony and reception settings?

- Will alterations be required? If so, who will make them?
- What is the cost of alterations?
- Are headpieces included?
- What is the cost of accessories? (shoes, undergarments, gloves, etc.)
- What is the total cost?

Men's Attire: Worry-Free Hints

- Rent from a large rental company that has a huge stock of tuxedos on hand. Do not order from a catalog at a bridal salon.
- Place the order at least three months before the wedding.
- Designate the best man to be in charge of seeing to it that all the men go into the shop to be measured by the date specified and to pick up the tuxedos before the wedding and return them after.

Men's Attire: Questions to Ask

- Is the tuxedo complementary to the bride's gown and the wedding's theme?
- When should the men come in to be measured?
- Will alterations be required? If so, who will make them?
- What is the cost of alterations?
- What is the cost of accessories? (shoes, vests, cummerbunds, shirt studs, cuff links, shirts, etc.)
- What is the total cost?

Mothers' Attire: Worry-Free Hints

- The mother of the bride purchases her dress first and then furnishes a fabric sample and photo of the dress to the mother of the groom.
- Encourage both mothers to purchase their gowns as soon as possible, because one of the biggest problems can be the mother who has procrastinated until the last minute.

Mothers' Attire: Questions to Ask

- Is the dress complementary to the bride's gown and the wedding's theme?
- Will alterations be required? If so, who will make them?
- What is the cost of alterations?

- What is the cost of accessories? (shoes, undergarments, jewelry, etc.)
- What is the total cost?

Junior Attendants' Attire: Worry-Free Hints

- If the groom's junior attendants will be wearing tuxedos, see "Men's Attire," on the preceding page for hints and questions.
- The attire for the bride's flower girl and/or junior attendants will be the responsibility of their parents, who should follow the same hints and questions listed above under "Bridesmaids' Attire."
- Encourage the mothers to have their daughters' dresses purchased or sewn at least six weeks before the wedding to avoid any last-minute problems.

Flowers: Worry-Free Hints

- Hire a professional florist or floral designer. Although an amateur florist may save you money, there can be last-minute hassles unless you're depending on a professional who does this type of thing all the time.
- As I already mentioned earlier in this chapter, you can avoid a lot of stress by ordering one of the standard wedding packages offered by the florist.
- Reserve your florist at least six months prior to the wedding date, or as soon as possible.
- Designate someone to go with you when you place your order and to stay in touch with the florist between now and the wedding, just to be sure everything is still on track and that there are no problems.

Flowers: Questions to Ask

- Name, address, telephone number and name of contact person?
- Which floral plan have I selected?
- Exactly what does this plan include? (number of bouquets, corsages, boutonnieres, table arrangements, etc., plus exactly what type and how many flowers will be used for each)
- What equipment does the florist provide? (wedding arch, aisle runner, pew holders or pew candlesticks)
- When will the flowers be delivered?
- What is the total cost?

Musicians: Worry-Free Hints

• If possible, eavesdrop on other weddings and observe each musician ahead of time before signing on the dotted line. This includes organist, soloists, harpist, DJs, stringed trios or dance bands. If this isn't possible, ask to be furnished with an audio- or videotape of their live performances.

• Hire professionals if at all possible.

• Book the musicians at least six months before the wedding, and furnish any sheet music necessary several months before the wedding, which will give the musicians time to practice.

• Take your designated helper with you when you book your musicians, then put that person in charge of staying in contact with each one between now and the wedding. (Hint, hint: This is a great job for your fiancé!)

Musicians: Questions to Ask

• What are your fees?

• If this is a DJ or a dance band, how many hours of music will be provided for this fee?

• If this is a dance band, how many members are there in the band?

• What kind of equipment will be furnished by the musician(s), and what will you need to furnish?

• Will any sheet music be required, or tapes or CDs for the DJ?

Photographer and Videographer: Worry-Free Hints

• Hire *only* professionals.

• Ask to view their work before hiring them.

• Hire the photographer as soon as you become engaged because you will need to have your engagement photo taken right away.

• Order one of their package wedding plans.

• Take your designated helper with you when you book your photographer and videographer, and put that person in charge of staying in contact with each between now and the wedding.

Photographer and Videographer: Questions to Ask

• Names, addresses and telephone numbers of each?

• Exactly what does the photographer's package plan include? (number of proofs, formal portrait fee, album costs, number and sizes of finished prints, costs for additional prints, number of hours "on duty," number of "candids," etc.)

• Exactly what does the videographer's package plan include? (number of hours "on duty," number of taped hours, type and number of battery packs, etc.)

• What is the total cost of each plan?

Transportation: Worry-Free Hints

• Limousine companies seem to have a heavy turnover of personnel, so keep in close touch with yours, confirming the date and the arrangements.

Transportation: Questions to Ask

• Exactly what does their fee include?

• How many hours of service are covered?

• Is there an ice bucket with champagne for the bride and groom on the ride from the ceremony site to the reception site?

• Is there a uniformed driver?

Decorations, Favors and Incidentals: Worry-Free Hints

• Even though these may seem like small things that can be done at any time, try to take care of them as soon as the wedding theme has been chosen. Believe me, this will prevent no end of last-minute anxiety and worry!

• Enlist the help of your "craftiest" friend to gather together everything needed to make the decorations and the favors, including a group of volunteers who are able to get together for an afternoon or evening to tie pew bows and to make the favors and any other decorations required.

• You can purchase ready-made favors and avoid *all* the hassles of making them.

Decorations, Favors and Incidentals: Questions to Ask

• What materials will be required to make the favors, if that is what you decide to do?

• What other decorations will be required for the ceremony and reception sites, including foyers, powder rooms and exteriors, such as driveways, walkways and entry doors?

Items to be Rented, Borrowed or Purchased: Worry-Free Hints

• Always rent or purchase an item rather than depend on someone furnishing something they have promised.

• Assign two volunteers to take care of these items: one responsible to pick up and return any rented or borrowed items and one to purchase the rest.

Items to be Rented, Borrowed or Purchased: Questions to Ask

• What needs to be provided at the ceremony and reception sites? (aisle runner, cake server, guest book and pen, ring bearer's pillow, tables and chairs, tablecloths, table skirts, kitchen equipment, table service, serving bowls and platters, trellises, helium tank, kneeling bench, waterfall, child's swimming pool(s), live or silk plants or flowering plants, arches, arbors, portable gazebo, portable tent(s), portable dance floor, Tiki torches, balloons, candles, etc.)

• Which of these items will be rented, and which will be purchased?

• What is the total cost?

Donate one full page in your notebook for each of the categories described above, including the "Worry-Free Hints," answers to questions asked and the name, address and telephone number of the person who is in charge of following up on each.

Worry-Free Wedding Day

If you follow the advice I have given so far, you should have an enjoyable, relaxed, worry-free engagement period, free of any last-minute anxieties and hassles—which brings us to the wedding day itself.

I *strongly* recommend that you arrange for a wedding day coordinator to ensure a worry-free wedding day as well. You can enlist the services of someone you know who has experience along this line or, better yet, hire a professional.

Here is what a wedding day coordinator can do to assure a worry-free day for you and your family:

At the Ceremony Site:

• Arrives early and checks the florist's delivery to be sure everything is there (the most common thing missing from a florist's order is the bride's throwaway bouquet). Then, she makes sure all the floral arrangements are in their proper places, the bouquets are delivered to the bride's dressing room and the boutonnieres are pinned on the men.

• Makes sure the members of the wedding party are "well put together," with no loose cummerbunds, unbuttoned collars or hosiery runs.

• Makes sure the guest book and pen are in place.

• Makes her emergency kit available to any members of the family or wedding party who may need it. (The emergency kit should include aspirin, sewing kit, first-aid kit, makeup kit, curling iron, hair spray and accessories, nail file and nail polish, glue, tape, hammer, sanitary products, tissues, smelling salts, safety pins, scissors, stapler, antacid tablets and several extra pairs of panty hose in various sizes.)

• Assembles the family and members of the wedding party for any preceremony photographs.

• Tries to keep everyone relaxed and happy by encouraging them to breathe and to smile!

• Greets the guests as they arrive and encourages them to sign the guest book.

• Makes sure the attendants are lined up in the proper order for the processional.

At the Reception Site

• Checks with the caterer to be sure everything is ready and that there are no problems.

• Checks with the DJ or the musicians to be sure they are ready and that they have a list of the order of events, including the dance order.

• Makes sure the tables are set for the correct number of guests and that the place cards are set properly at any reserved tables.

• Makes sure the bride's train is bustled or removed at the beginning of the reception.

• If there is no receiving line, makes sure the bride and groom have a chance to visit personally with every guest by escorting them from table to table off and on during the reception.

• Signals to the videographer and photographer when it is time for any special event, such as the first dance, the father-daughter dance, the toasts, the cutting of the cake, the bouquet toss, the garter toss, etc., and generally makes sure the reception runs on schedule.

• Makes sure all gift envelopes are kept in a secure place.

• Monitors the volume of the music.

• Handles any little problems that may arise, shielding the couple and their families from any possible wedding day stress.

• Distributes any checks payable to wedding vendors at the end of the reception.

• Signals to the ushers or groomsmen when it's time to carry the wedding gifts to a designated vehicle.

• After the bride and groom have left the reception, returns with the couple's parents to be sure nothing has been left behind anywhere on the site, including the rest rooms and dressing rooms.

There's bound to be some little thing that goes wrong on your wedding day, but it will probably be something totally insignificant, such as the time a bridesmaid forgot her dyed-to-match teal-blue shoes at home a thousand miles away. She wore a pair of grey pumps she borrowed from the bride's mother, and did it really matter? Of course not! In fact, they were barely noticeable in the photos!

Remember, as long as you end your day as husband and wife, it has been an absolutely perfect wedding day!

Tiffany and Michael Gray

This is the story of Tiffany and Mike who were married on September 21, 1996, in Santa Barbara, California, in a wedding that, thanks to careful planning and the help of their friends and family, was almost totally worry-free.

Mike and Tiffany met during their senior year at college when they were both involved with the United Way campaign on campus. She was the coordinator of fund raising from the staff and alumni, and he was in charge of student contributions. Their goal was to receive *some* kind of a contribution from every single person, even if only a token amount. They wanted to be able to say that their campus had contributed 100 percent.

This monumental effort resulted in four months of "togetherness," where—you guessed it—they became attracted to each other and started dating. By graduation week they were engaged to be married the following September.

Mike said, "I can't believe she was here all the time—if I hadn't volunteered to help with the United Way campaign, I might have never met her!"

With only three and a half months to plan their wedding, here are a few of the things that kept the planning as relaxed and uncomplicated as possible.

Ceremony and Reception Site: Tiffany and Mike set their wedding date based on which Saturday Tiffany's church was available. The formal ceremony took place in the main sanctuary and the reception in the adjacent rose garden.

Theme: The rose garden, with its array of pink rose bushes, inspired the wedding's theme. Pink roses were used in the sanctuary, in the women's bouquets, as boutonnieres, in bud vases on each table in the garden and as decoration on the wedding cake.

Bride's Gown: Tiffany, her mother and sister drove to Los

Angeles to attend a Saturday bridal show, where Tiffany purchased a gown she liked, one of several hundred on display by a local wedding vendor. It was a short-sleeved gown with a sweetheart neckline and low back from the Eden Collection. It fit perfectly and needed no alterations.

Attendants' Gowns: Two weeks later Tiffany and her five attendants spent the day in Los Angeles, where they found dresses at Macy's. They were sleeveless silk sheaths with side slits in a "cotton candy shade of pink." Fortunately, they were able to purchase one in each of the women's sizes. Only one of the dresses required an alteration.

Men's Attire: Mike handled the ordering of tuxedos for all the men—an all-white ensemble by Oscar de la Renta.

Flower Girl's Dress: Once the attendants had purchased their dresses, fabric was purchased in the same color to be used as a sash for a white confirmation dress that was purchased for the flower girl. She carried a white basket filled with pink rose petals.

Caterer: An excellent caterer was hired on the recommendation of the church organist, who was familiar with all the local catering services. They chose the Light Afternoon Luncheon Buffet, which included finger sandwiches, several salads, spinach dip, fruit kabobs and relish trays. The food was displayed at food stations scattered around the garden, one table for each type of food, plus a cake table and a drink table. The catering company also provided cake cutters and servers.

Wedding Cake: The cake was ordered from a local bakery from a photograph in their display album. It was composed of four layers that stood on separate glass podiums. The frosting was applied in a wicker basket design, and each layer was topped with fresh pink rose buds, along with roses and ivy that encircled the bottom of each layer. It was exquisite and complemented the formality of the Rose Garden theme.

Flowers, Decorations and Favors: A talented friend of Tiffany's mom took charge of these three things. She asked Tiffany what style bouquet she wanted for herself and her bridesmaids, then she met with the florist and placed the entire order herself. She also assembled several friends who tied the pew bows and wrapped jars of bubble-blowing liquid in pink satin fabric and ribbon. These decorated jars were given to the guests during the reception to be used to blow bubbles at the bride and groom as they made their getaway.

This terrific lady also rented white folding chairs to go with the fifteen round tables that belonged to the church, plus eight round patio tables with large white umbrellas. The umbrella poles were wound with pink ribbon like a maypole from the bottom up, with streamers of ribbon dangling down from the top.

Photographer: The photographer was recommended by the caterer (who had been recommended by the church organist). Tiffany and Mike chose one of his basic packages with the option of ordering more prints at a later date.

Videographer: Mike took charge of locating a reputable videographer.

Musicians: The church organist was hired to play during the ceremony, in addition to a soloist who sang "The Wedding Song" to taped accompaniment and a harpist who performed during the seating of the guests. Mike knew of three talented music students from the university who were hired as a string trio to play throughout the reception. Tiffany's dad offered to pay for white tuxes for these three men, which enhanced their classical performance.

Near the end of the reception, Tiffany's father and three of his friends, all members of a local barbershop quartet, surprised everyone with two songs: "Let Me Call You Sweetheart" and "How Ya Gonna Keep 'Em Down on the Farm," which had lyrics personalized to tell Tiffany and Mike's love story.

Wedding Day Coordinator: There was no official wedding day coordinator, but Tiffany's aunt and uncle, who served as host and hostess of the reception, kept things running smoothly and on schedule.

Transportation: Because the ceremony and reception were held at the same site, it wasn't necessary to arrange for transportation between sites, but Tiffany's dad insisted on an elegant white horse-drawn carriage as the getaway vehicle. The carriage drew cheers from people along the two-mile route from the church to the Inn on Summer Hill by the Sea, where Mike and Tiffany's honeymoon abode awaited. It had an ocean view, a fireplace and an in-room whirlpool. Their one-night stay was a wedding gift from Mike's grandparents, and then they left the next day for their ten-day Maui honeymoon.

Mike and Tiffany's wedding plans were made in less than four months with a minimal amount of stress and anxiety. There were several reasons for this, the most important being that the church doubled as ceremony and reception site, and the rose garden dictated the wedding's theme. Also, because Mike took care of hiring the videographer and reserving the men's tuxes, and the friend of Tiffany's mom took charge of the flowers and decorations, the only vendors Tiffany had to meet with were the caterer, the bakery and the photographer. Tiffany said, "Everything else just seemed to fall into place."

Of course, it didn't hurt that the women lucked out and were able to purchase their dresses off the rack and that there were no special-order requests for the florist, photographer, bakery or catering service.

Wouldn't it be nice if all do-it-yourself weddings could be this relaxed and trouble-free? ♡

If this chapter has given you a "Yes! I can do it!" feeling, that's great! If, however, even after my best worry-free advice, it still seems like an overwhelming task, you may want to consider hiring a professional bridal consultant. The next chapter will help you understand how helpful one of these wedding specialists can be as you read the case histories of weddings they have planned.

THINGS TO REMEMBER:

○ As you plan your wedding, don't forget to *breathe*. A long, slow, deep breath is a luxurious pleasure. Don't deprive yourself!

○ Running away from home is a great escape from the stress of planning your wedding, even if only for a few hours at a time.

○ Every wedding has *some* little thing that goes wrong, but as long as you end the big day as husband and wife, what difference does it really make?

○ Even though you're busy with the planning, try to work some strenuous exercise into each day—ride your bike up a hill, challenge your fiancé to a game of racquetball or just take off on a long-distance run.

○ Turn off the lights, turn off the phone, light a scented candle and sink down into a hot tub full of bubbles. Great relaxation technique!

○ READ THE FINE PRINT BEFORE SIGNING ANY CONTRACTS!

○ Don't talk about your wedding plans *all* the time—you'll wear everyone out, including yourself!

○ Treat yourself to a professional massage every few weeks before the wedding—you deserve it! To locate a Certified Massage Therapist in your area, call the National Certification Board for Therapeutic Massage at (800) 296-0664.

CHAPTER SIX

The Professionally Planned Wedding

CASE STUDIES FROM MASTER BRIDAL CONSULTANTS

I t is an honor for me to present case histories contributed by Master Bridal Consultants of the Association of Bridal Consultants, a highly respected organization whose members agree to uphold high standards and subscribe to a strict code of ethics and who have demonstrated professional competency in a number of ways.

Let me tell you a little bit about this organization. It has approximately 1,500 members who have been awarded certificates based on their participation in professional seminars, recognition by peers and clients and completion of proficiency examinations. The association has three designations:

- Professional Bridal Consultant
- Accredited Bridal Consultant
- Master Bridal Consultant

It is not easy to reach the designation of Professional Bridal Consultant, but it is even more difficult to reach the next two. There are only twenty-one Accredited Bridal Consultants in the organization and fewer than ten members who have reached the highest level, Master Bridal Consultant.

These Master Bridal Consultants are the *crème de la crème*. To be awarded this rare designation, a member must achieve the following:

- Be a member for a minimum of six years
- Successfully pass advanced proficiency examinations
- Participate in professional association seminars or workshops
- Be recommended by a minimum number of peers and clients

They must also achieve at least one of the following:

- Publication of a wedding-related story, book, etc.

- Presentation of a wedding-related seminar or other educational program
- Participation in an electronic media event (radio or television talk show or a feature program)
- Served as an Association State Coordinator for at least one year

You can see why it is not easy to become a Master Bridal Consultant, so it's no wonder less than one percent of the membership has been awarded this highly respected designation. I'm sure you will find their case histories, as well as their free professional advice, interesting and helpful.

Mary Rahal, Master Bridal Consultant
Waldorf Engraving and Printing, Waldorf, Maryland

Mary Rahal provided an excellent example of how a professional bridal consultant can make a wedding worry-free. Her motto is "A Hassle-Free Wedding."

Here is one of her case histories as told by the bride herself.

CASE HISTORY # 1

John and Tammy Beavers

We are John and Tammy Beavers and we would like to tell you about our wonderful wedding day. First, however, I think you should know a little bit about us.

We are both from a rural community south of Washington, DC, known as Southern Maryland. We met while volunteering at a local fire department. I was on summer vacation from college, and John was at the community college studying for his paramedic's license. Our relationship began as a summer romance, but it continued as a long-distance romance when I returned to college. We dated for three years, and during that time I began medical school at Georgetown University in Washington, DC, while John began working there as a paramedic. We fell in love quickly and spent almost all our free time together.

In the fall of 1994 John and I decided that it was time to make more permanent plans for ourselves. John proposed to me on Thursday, October 20, 1994. I had just finished class that evening, and John was waiting for me. He told me he was taking me to dinner at one of our favorite outdoor, waterfront restaurants downtown. As we sat outside watching the sun set, he pulled out a beautiful diamond ring and proposed to me.

We knew our lives were anything but "normal." We both spent long, crazy hours at work, including nights. I was training to become a doctor and John was a paramedic, so we also knew it would be difficult to squeeze time out of our schedules to make wedding plans. I wanted an October wedding, but I knew I would have more flexibility in my schedule during my last year of medical school, so the date was set for October 1996.

Mary Rahal entered our lives via my mother. Several of her colleagues at work had recommended Mary. My mother realized I needed a wedding coordinator when she saw how I was struggling with the phone book to make calls to reception sites for four hours one afternoon. Also, because I lived seventy miles away in Washington, DC, it was difficult planning a wedding long distance.

From the first time I met Mary I knew she would be a great resource. She sat down with me and my mother and talked over everything we would need to do to put on this wedding. She had terrific ideas about what would work for the festive, party-type wedding I wanted.

CEREMONY AND RECEPTION SITES

I had already chosen my hometown church for the ceremony, but the reception site was a chore to locate. I had tentatively booked the local fire department social hall. Mary, however, suggested several other locations I hadn't thought of, including the Olde Breton Inn, an old house overlooking Breton Bay that has been converted into a banquet facility.

The Olde Breton Inn is known for its catering service, and the staff provided us with a beautifully prepared buffet, including a magnificent ice sculpture created by one of the owners. They also provided an open bar for a reasonable fee and even allowed us to book the entire evening without an extra charge.

On the day of the wedding the reception site was classy but relaxed, and the food was outstanding. My mother and I received compliments for weeks after the wedding.

VENDORS

The flower arrangements were a challenge from the beginning. I had no sense of flowers, so I needed someone I could trust to do a good job. Mary highly recommended a local florist who graciously booked our wedding over the phone a year in advance without having met us.

When I finally met the florist, I told her what colors I wanted in the bouquets and left it all up to her. The day of the wedding was the first time I saw my bouquets, and they were stunning.

John and I wanted a DJ for the reception, and the one Mary recommended was wonderful. He went out of his way to be sure he had the songs we requested, even though he had to purchase some of them a few days before the wedding. He wanted John and me to relax and have a good time at our wedding, and he made it a point to meet us at the limo with drinks when we arrived. He also had a wonderful way of getting people out on the dance floor, and he truly helped create the fun, party atmosphere John and I wanted.

Mary recommended a local woman who I had heard made terrific cakes. When John and I met her and sampled her work, she definitely lived up to her reputation. Our wedding cake had five layers, each a different flavor, fanned out as if the layers were steps in a semi-circular staircase. When I told her I wanted fresh flowers on my cake, she said it was no problem. She assured me that she and the florist often worked out an arrival schedule at the reception site so that the cake and flowers were both fresh and in place on time.

My photographer also came highly recommended by Mary and by several of my mother's friends. The day of the wedding he was completely professional and very inconspicuous. Many guests commented on how they forgot the photographer was even there.

My mother and I had visited several bridal shops locally and in Washington, DC, but Mary suggested one local shop in particular because, in her experience, it provided exceptional customer service. When I went there to look at dresses, the employees really focused on service and tried to work with my preferences to find a gown as close to my ideal vision as possible. After several visits the owner brought out a brand-new arrival that was everything I had hoped for.

My invitations, thank-you notes and paper goods were purchased through Mary's printing company, Waldorf Engraving and Printing. Needless to say they were perfect. When the stationery arrived, Mary personally inspected every single sheet for typos and smudges before calling to say they were ready.

FINAL PLANNING

As we got closer to the wedding day, Mary met with us to work out last-minute details and scheduling. She brought up things I would never have considered on my own, such as reserving seating for family, deciding how to announce and seat John's stepparents correctly, and making sure the timing would be just right so John and I could enjoy our day.

At the rehearsal Mary made sure all details were covered, but she did not become intrusive while the priest was going over his plans for the rehearsal.

The day of the wedding Mary was completely professional. She was also prepared for any possible calamity with her bag of tricks, including food in case we forgot to eat, umbrellas in case a freak storm occurred and tissues in case anyone forgot. She also brought lots of other odds and ends that she had learned over years of experience to have on hand.

During the reception she discreetly made sure that John and I stayed on schedule while still having a good time. She even arranged for our ushers to remove our gifts near the end of the reception and pack them into my parents' car.

Needless to say, our wedding day was perfect and went off without any problems. Mary was such a great help and made it possible for my family, as well as John and me, to enjoy our wedding day to the fullest. ♡

Jo Ann Swofford, Master Bridal Consultant
That Special Touch, Berryville, Arkansas

Although Jo Ann's company, That Special Touch, is located in Berryville, she is actually a destination wedding planner for the nearby town of Eureka Springs. I say "town," but it is barely a village. With a population of less than two thousand, Eureka Springs hosts over three thousand weddings each year, and there is a very good reason why: Known as "The Little Switzerland of the Ozarks," this tiny village is not only a romantic place to get married, but it also offers honeymooners a lover's paradise with its wraparound forests, freshwater lakes, natural springs and tranquilizing views. Its busy little downtown is full of antique shops, historical B&Bs, crafts stores and art galleries, and less than an hour away a world of entertainment is available in Branson, Missouri.

Jo Ann is a busy lady, planning weddings just as fast as she can! And here's the story of one of them.

CASE HISTORY # 2

Daniel and Sandra Milam

I had never heard so many successful "blind date stories" until I started putting this book together. Here's another one. Daniel and Sandra met on a blind date set up by mutual friends. (I've come to the conclusion that mutual friends make excellent matchmakers!)

Their date went so well that they saw each other every day after that until two months later when Daniel asked Sandra to marry him. Well, he didn't exactly *ask* her to marry him, but he did say, "I want to get married." Sandra said that she didn't know if he expected an answer or if he was simply making a statement, but it was good enough for her, and she said, "Yes."

On a trip to Eureka Springs, Daniel and Sandy decided this was definitely the place they wanted to exchange their vows. Once that decision was made, Sandy thought the planning would be easy. She would just get a few names of vendors, make a few calls and everything would be set up. However, after attempting to contact some of the hotels in Eureka Springs to book a reception location, she was at her wit's end. Not one hotel returned her call!

CHOOSING A BRIDAL CONSULTANT

In looking through some materials from the Eureka Springs Chamber of Commerce, Sandra came across the name of Jo Ann's company, That Special Touch. She was hesitant to call at first but was later glad she did. She said, "I was shocked by the response I received because Jo Ann was so helpful, returned my calls and answered all my questions. Within minutes, I decided that I couldn't plan my wedding without someone's help, and this lady named Jo Ann was more than willing. In the time span of one week, I had my reception hall booked, all the arrangements made, my cake ordered and all the small details taken care of."

Jo Ann told me, "Sandy was still hesitant even after all the arrangements we had made for her. After all, I was only a name and a voice at the end of a telephone. She was, to say the least, a tad nervous. I tried my best to assure her that I had planned hundreds of weddings and never had a bride who was displeased."

When Daniel and Sandy arrived four days before the wedding, Sandy said, "I had nothing to worry about—Jo Ann had taken care of everything."

Daniel and Sandy's wedding budget was $3,000, and they expected seventy-five guests, but that was no problem for Jo Ann. She had booked a beautiful glass wedding chapel in the woods that was just the perfect size and had contracted with a local hotel that had a lovely room for the hors d'oeuvres-and-cake reception. The cake was chosen from photographs sent to Sandy in advance, and the food and cake together totaled only $1,700. In addition, there was an open bar with a $500 limit. (After the limit, guests were able to purchase any drinks of their choice.)

FLOWERS AND DECORATIONS

Sandy chose to make her own bouquet of silk flowers. She also sent Jo Ann a few extra flowers ahead of time to help match colors for the tulle and bows that were added to greenery around the candelabra at the chapel. The reception site was decorated in the same colors, as well.

Finally, after all was said and done, Sandy and Daniel had the wedding of their dreams, photography and all, for just under their $3,000 limit.

Sandy said, "My wedding day was flawless—Jo Ann is the perfect coordinator for any wedding."

What a difference it makes to have an experienced bridal consultant on your side! ♡

Sue Winner, Master Bridal Consultant
Sue Winner and Associates, Atlanta, Georgia

Sue Winner, owner of Sue Winner and Associates, shared the story of Nona and Kevin Taitz. Sue's first contact regarding planning Nona and Kevin's wedding came from Nona's mother, Margie Friedman. Mrs. Friedman explained that she and her daughter currently lived in Florida, but that Nona was being transferred to Georgia in the future. And because Kevin lived in Georgia, they wanted to hold the wedding in Atlanta.

Because Sue made most of the arrangements for the wedding via long distance with the help of Nona's parents, Nona and Kevin's story is told from that perspective.

Nona and Kevin Taitz

Kevin's friend was dating Nona's roommate and had planned to have Kevin and Nona meet. Before he had a chance to "fix them up," however, Kevin and Nona just happened to meet while playing pool at a bar. They hit it off right away and "knew pretty quickly" they were meant for each other. Kevin proposed to Nona during a romantic hansom cab ride through Manhattan's Central Park.

CEREMONY AND RECEPTION SITE

By the time Sue was under contract to plan the wedding, Margie, Nona's mother, had already secured the Swissôtel in Atlanta as the ceremony and reception site. The groom's family had already secured a rabbi to perform the Jewish ceremony, and the time of the ceremony was already established to conform to Jewish law regarding the Sabbath.

Sue asked Margie a series of questions about her tastes and desires for the musical selections for her daughter's wedding, and from this Sue determined that Nona would be happiest with live music, probably a band of four to six pieces. Sue faxed a list of four or five bands to Margie that she believed Nona would like and would be within her budget requests. Then, Margie contacted each group and asked the leaders several questions before requesting an audio- or videotape of each group's performances.

When the tapes arrived, Nona, Margie and Harris, the bride's father, narrowed down their choices. Sue explained the importance of actually observing each band playing at a wedding, preferably a Jewish wedding, since the timing and flow of a Jewish wedding is somewhat different than an American Protestant or Catholic wedding.

Before contracting with one of the bands, Nona made arrangements to see each one in performance as soon as she moved to Atlanta. She asked each one to hold her wedding date on their schedule until she could view them in person. The same arrangements were made with the photographer and videographer.

When Nona moved to Atlanta, she and Kevin finally met with Sue face to face. Nona came in to order her wedding gown through Sue's connection with Discount Bridal Service, Inc.

SELECTION OF VENDORS

Nona selected a band after listening to three groups' live performances, and she selected a videographer after reviewing videotapes of his work. She also visited photographers and made her choice. It was then Sue was consulted about the various vendors' contracts. Although Sue is not an attorney, she does look for any awkwardly worded phrases that may cause ambiguity or misunderstandings. Then she suggests phrasings that are not only clearer but that also protect the client.

In very short order, contracts were signed with the band, the photographer, the videographer and the ceremony musicians. The caterer came with the ceremony/reception facility, so that was already under control.

The florist took somewhat more time to finalize. Sue suggested four or five florists—most of whom were floral designers, rather than floral shops. Then she read the proposals and suggested ways the costs could be cut without making a major impact on the appearance of the wedding. Soon that proposal/contract was signed as well.

Margie and Sue spoke frequently about etiquette, logistics and such things as transportation, how to address envelopes, programs to notify guests of the weekend activities and the hotels where blocks of rooms had been booked at special discounted rates for the wedding.

FINAL PLANNING

Six weeks before the wedding Sue met with Nona and her parents to plan the wedding in detail. During this meeting Margie and Harris decided they wanted the guests to receive "welcome baskets" when they checked into their hotels, and they wanted them to have a Georgian theme. Sue offered to create these baskets herself with *peach* salsas, *peach*-shaped nacho chips, *pecan* rolls, *peanuts*, *peanut butter* crackers, and, of course, *Coca-Cola*, all products of Georgia.

During this meeting, a questionnaire was completed, and from it Sue was able to write a detailed script of the wedding, listing every wish the parents and the bride had expressed. Sue mailed an abbreviated version of this script to every vendor ten days before the wedding, sharing the family's likes and dislikes, with follow-up phone calls a few days before the wedding, offering to help the vendors with any equipment or logistics problems. She also sent letters to the bride and groom and their families that listed times, locations and any checks that needed to be prepared in advance and brought to the wedding in sealed envelopes.

During the rehearsal on Friday afternoon she gave everyone their individual instructions as to walking into the ceremony, where to stand, what to do with their hands, how to turn, who to walk out with, and so forth. She then explained to the couple and their parents that from the end of the rehearsal until the wedding itself, she would be on twenty-four-hour call to run errands, pick up forgotten items, or to do whatever else was needed.

THE WEDDING AND RECEPTION

Sue arrived at the wedding four hours before the ceremony was scheduled, along with her four-foot-tall rolling cart with four drawers filled with emergency equipment to repair almost anything that could go wrong. (She even carries a miniature sewing machine!)

After steaming the wedding gown and bridesmaids' dresses, she pinned boutonnieres on the men and then set the scene for the photographer by "staging" the first time the groom would see his bride in her gown. Finally, she met with the caterer, videographer, florist and musicians to be sure everything was in order.

Soon the ceremony music began and the wedding was under way. Standing in the back watching the ceremony and the families' great happiness, she blotted a tear of joy, as she always does!

Sue remained at the wedding through the cocktail reception,

making sure the tables were arranged according to the room diagram and that they were set for the correct number of guests. Then, as the couple was introduced, she checked with the caterer, band leader, photographer and videographer to make sure everything was going well.

From the moment Sue arrived four hours before the ceremony until the end of the reception, she was on duty for seven hours—and not a single problem occurred during that entire time.

By the way, when I had a chance to speak with the bride and groom personally, Kevin confirmed how well everything went and that he definitely recommends hiring a professional bridal consultant. ♡

Cheri Rice, Master Bridal Consultant
The Personal Touch Bridal Agency,
Anoka, Minnesota

Cheri decided to share Peter and Kylie's story, not only because their wedding was wonderful, but because it had so many interesting twists, such as the trolley car that was used to bring the guests from the church to the reception.

Another interesting aspect of this wedding was that it had to be planned long distance since the bride was living in Indiana during most of the planning period.

CASE HISTORY # 4

Peter and Kylie Wiltjer

Peter and Kylie met at Valparaiso University at a combined party sponsored by her sorority and his fraternity. Peter asked Kylie for her last name so he could call her. Then the next day they just happened to bump into each other at a concert and were a "bit intrigued by each other." They started seeing each other and dated for about three years before they got engaged.

Peter says he fell in love with Kylie when he met up with her at the concert the day after the party. Kylie fell in love with Peter "because of the person he is that most people don't see—like the way he is with his family, and his sharp sense of humor that makes me want to laugh, and when he took me home to visit his family over Easter weekend."

Peter and Kylie planned to celebrate a quiet Valentine's Day dinner at Kylie's apartment, but when she got home from work that day, there was a cassette tape in her mailbox with a note that said "Play me." She played the tape, which was the Beatles' song "When I'm 64." Kylie thought it was great and wondered what Peter was implying. She didn't dare get her hopes up that it could mean an engagement in case he just meant the song as a sentiment.

Then, over dinner, Peter asked Kylie to marry him as he presented her with an engagement ring. Kylie was enormously surprised—not only that Peter proposed to her, but that he gave her a ring, for she had never even been fitted for a ring. Peter had had a new diamond set into his grandmother's platinum engagement ring and then had it sized a little smaller than his pinky. He'd remembered that an old class ring of his that fit his pinky had fit Kylie's finger just right. Smart guy, that Peter!

Because Kylie needed to plan her wedding in less than five months from a distance of five hundred miles away, she sought out Cheri's assistance at her mother's suggestion. Actually, the entire wedding was planned during Kylie's brief one-week visit home over spring break. Cheri had made all the calls and appointments in advance, so all Kylie had to do was visit with the vendors while she was home. She saw three florists one day, three photographers another, and so on. By the end of Kylie's visit, all the decisions had been made, the wedding had been planned and she returned to Indiana knowing Cheri would carry through with everything.

CEREMONY AND RECEPTION SITES

The ceremony was held in Kylie's home church in Minnesota, and the reception was in the backyard of her parents' beautifully restored farmhouse, which sits on a lake. Kylie's parents spent many hours landscaping the yard for the occasion, including the addition of a rock wall and planting new flowers. The setting was perfect for a wedding reception because of its large wooden deck for dancing, white lattice arbor that "framed" the band, and a balcony that was ideal for the bouquet toss.

The trees and a large white tent were outlined with tiny white lights, and the interior of the tent was decorated with flowers and greenery. The tables were set with large bubble bowls filled with floating candles and flowers.

Some of the best memories of the wedding day were created by the use of a trolley car and a motorcoach to ferry the guests from the church to the reception. The guests loved it—they sang songs and got to know each other. Then, as the guests wanted to leave, the trolley car took them to their hotels or back to their cars at the church. The family had wondered how they would ever park 150 cars along the narrow road by Kylie's parents' home, but this was the perfect solution.

Kylie's brother, Tyler, designed the ceremony program as a wedding gift, creating a collage of words and pictures. The programs were printed on recycled paper in black and off-white. Kylie and her mother created a helpful newsletter and map for the out-of-town guests that gave directions from the airport and a list of sites to see in the area along with sightseeing brochures.

WEDDING ATTIRE

Kylie wore an ivory shantung floor-length gown with off-the-shoulder long sleeves that were detachable in case the outdoor reception turned warm, which it did. Her attendants and flower girls wore blue tea-length dresses.

Peter wore a black tuxedo with a shawl collar and tails, an ivory shirt and a vest. His groomsmen, ushers and ring bearer wore the same style black tuxedos, but with cummerbunds instead of vests.

Kylie did her own hair for the wedding, but she indulged in a professional manicure two days before, which she said was "a very nice, relaxing treat." Her good friend, Anne, who was also one of her attendants, is a makeup artist and contributed her talents to the cause as well.

Peter's mother purchased a lace bag that was worn by Kylie's cousin during the reception. This was where all the gift envelopes were placed—nice and safe all evening long!

THE RECEPTION

Because the reception began immediately after the ceremony, the wedding party and family members had all their photos taken before the ceremony began. They also had a videographer who taped the ceremony and reception, which was especially nice because copies could be sent to those who weren't able to travel to the wedding.

The reception began with butler-served hors d'oeuvres and champagne, followed by a hot two-meat buffet plus several side dishes, including wild rice, artichoke salad and fruit kabobs. In addition to the wedding cake, which was raspberry-filled with white frosting and decorated with green ivy and bright flowers, there were heart-shaped cookies and strawberries with chocolate sauce and cream.

Live music was provided all night long. During the receiving line, the cocktail hour and dinner, there was a roaming string trio, followed by a dance band later on.

The whole day went smoothly and Kylie gives all the credit to Cheri. Kylie told me, "Having someone else worry about the details took the pressure off and allowed us to focus on what we wanted our day to be. Because of Cheri, my mom didn't have to run around after the photographers and the florists—she could just relax and enjoy entertaining friends and family, which is how it should be. Actually, she got to enjoy the day as much as I did." ♡

Nancy DeProspo, Master Bridal Consultant
Humbug Associates, Greenacres, Florida

Although Nancy now lives and works in Greenacres, Florida, she was living and working in New Jersey when she planned the wedding for Michael and

Susan, which is featured below. She owned a company called Affairs of the Heart, a special event planning service located in Toms River, New Jersey.

The first time Nancy met the bride was at a wedding. Nancy relates, "Susan was an absolute delight to meet." Then, their professional paths crossed again when Nancy arranged a brunch seminar that was held at the bridal shop owned by Susan. Eventually, when Susan became engaged to Michael, she asked Nancy to be their wedding consultant. Here is the story of their wedding.

CASE HISTORY # 5

Susan and Michael Chao

Susan was with a friend at a nightclub called Montego Bay in Belmar, New Jersey, which she describes as "a summer hot spot for young adults," when Michael drove up in a Lamborghini Countach. When he stopped in front of the club, Susan's friend stepped forward to take a look at his sports car, and while she did, Michael and Susan struck up a conversation.

The following evening they went on a date. They took a boat to a restaurant called Wharfside that sat on the water. From that night on they never dated anyone but each other.

Susan said, "We fell in love by spending a lot of quality time together. We share many of the same interests—skiing, traveling to the Caribbean, going on cruises, spending time at the beach and casinos." She also said that they respect the time each spends on his or her own interests—Michael's love of tennis and exotic sports cars and Susan's love of exercising and shopping.

In April 1990 Michael and Susan went to Walt Disney World for their birthdays. They were at Pleasure Island, where every night is "New Year's Eve" with fireworks. Just before midnight Michael proposed to Susan as he gave her an engagement ring. Then the fireworks went off—what a great way to celebrate!

CHOOSING A BRIDAL CONSULTANT

Michael owns a computer business in Edison, New Jersey, and, although Susan currently works as a buyer and director of bridal sales for Kleinfeld Bridal Salon in Brooklyn, New York, she owned her own bridal salon at the time she was planning her wedding. Because they both owned their own businesses, neither one had the time to organize and keep track of their wedding plans. They decided they needed a bridal consultant to help them out, and Susan contacted Nancy.

TWO WEDDING CEREMONIES

Their first wedding ceremony was held at 2:30 in the afternoon at St. Mary's of the Lake in Lakewood, New Jersey. Then, because the reception was to be held an hour and a half drive north of the church and most of the guests lived close to that location, they decided to have a second ceremony at 6:30 P.M. at their reception site. This was a nondenominational service held in the garden of The Manor in West Orange, one of the most exclusive sites in New Jersey.

Because this is such an exclusive site, Nancy was a bit apprehensive about meeting and working with the banquet manager, since some banquet facilities of this caliber aren't very receptive to "outside advice." In this case, however, there was nothing but mutual respect from the start between Nancy and the banquet manager. He gave Nancy full rein, which, as she said, "is a nice feeling from such an established place." They even worked with her on the little things. For example, Susan's mother really wanted lemon slices in the water served to the guests at each table, which was no problem at all.

CHOOSING VENDORS

Between North and South Jersey lies a bridge spanning the Hudson River, and it has always been Nancy's impression that expenses are higher on the north side of the bridge. So although the reception was located in North Jersey, to save money Nancy drew most of the vendors from South Jersey. That way she could provide Michael and Susan with the wedding they wanted at a much lower cost than if the northern vendors had been used instead. Even so, the total cost of the wedding came in at $40,150! Imagine what it would have been if Nancy hadn't been able to draw from South Jersey.

Live music accompanied both ceremonies. An organist and a soloist provided the music for the first ceremony, and a three-piece string group performed during the second.

For the first ceremony the two head pews were decorated with bows and flowers, and white bows decorated the remaining pews. There were also two altar arrangements in addition to arrangements for the statues. White silk roses filled with birdseed and rose petals in a basket were provided to toss on the bride and groom for good luck.

At the garden ceremony, tulle garlands, bows and flowers decorated the white metal arches. The altar was decorated with roses and lilies, and the table centerpieces consisted of tiers of white lilies and pink roses surrounded by long tapered candles.

WEDDING ATTIRE

Susan's gown was a long-sleeved off-the-shoulder of white silk satin with a full cathedral-length train and two front pleats that created an overskirt look.

Because Michael is Chinese, Susan wanted to follow the Chinese custom of wearing a different gown for the reception, so during dinner she changed into a custom-designed white silk satin sheath with detachable train. Because she owned her own bridal shop, she was able to purchase her bridal gowns at wholesale prices: Her church ceremony gown cost her $1,500, and her reception ceremony gown $2,500. They must have been incredible!

The bridal attendants wore Watters and Watters pink silk shantung two-piece gowns with long, slim, slit-back skirts. Susan was able to purchase these seven gowns for a total wholesale price of $800. The flower girls wore dresses with white satin bodices, short puffed sleeves, long, full tulle skirts and back bows.

The groom and his groomsmen wore black double-breasted tuxedos with white shirts. The groom wore a black bow tie, and the groomsmen's were pink.

The bride and her attendants went to three different hair-styling salons simultaneously so they would all be back at the bride's home in time for their makeup to be applied by two makeup artists. Each of the women also received a French manicure the day before the wedding.

RECEPTION

The reception began with a cocktail hour at 7:00 P.M., followed by a prime rib of beef sit-down dinner for 175 guests. The cocktail hour featured buffet stations that offered pastas, stir-fry, seafood and an "endless array of selections." There was so much food, in fact, that many of the guests mistook it for "dinner." There was also a rolling bar service offered throughout the dinner hour, followed by a champagne toast.

The five-tiered cake had stairs adjoining two additional cakes, as well as a pink waterfall that flowed beneath the five tiers. The cake was decorated with pink ribbons and roses and a blown glass heart that formed the cake top. In addition to the wedding cake, there were also dessert stations throughout the room that offered cheesecakes, layer cakes, ice cream and, of course, fortune cookies!

Music was furnished by a DJ. The first dance was "Chances Are" followed by "After All," and the bride and her father danced to "Wind Beneath My Wings."

The bride sat for her formal bridal portrait one month before the wedding. This 16″ × 20″ portrait was displayed during the reception.

During the reception the bride was presented with a Barbie doll dressed in a handmade replica of the bridal gown, made from the same lace and beads as the bride's actual gown. The doll was enclosed in a glass and wood display case.

The guests were given boxed and wrapped cake servers, each with an engraved inscription.

During the reception Nancy made sure everything ran smoothly, checking to see that the favors were in place, each water glass had a slice of lemon, the bridal party stayed "intact," introductions were made and the guests were kept content. Finally, at the end of the reception, she made sure all the vendors were paid and the wedding gifts were loaded into her station wagon to be stored in her home until the bride and groom returned from their honeymoon.

The transportation was provided by four white limousines which were kept busy all day, including the trip from the first ceremony site to the second ceremony site! Eight rooms were booked at the Ramada Inn for the out-of-town attendants, and each room was furnished with a gift bag of snacks, candy, wine and cheese.

The wedding day was flawless, which is hard to believe—with two ceremonies an hour and a half drive apart, two bridal gowns, four limos and five tiers of wedding cake! Definitely not a "simple, little wedding," but a wonderful example of how a professional bridal consultant is able to coordinate a complicated wedding to perfection. ♡

Helen Louie, Master Bridal Consultant
Mother of the Bride, Sacramento, California

The name of Helen's company is Mother of the Bride, and the case history she has contributed is the story of Tom and Melina's wedding. The couple's last name is omitted at their request.

Their story is told from Helen's point of view.

CASE HISTORY # 6

Tom and Melina

I have chosen to tell you about Tom and Melina, probably because I like them as people, as well as the fact they had a very nice wedding. You could sense their mutual respect and depth of commitment.

Melina's cousin and her husband, Jason, introduced Tom and Melina. Tom and Melina discovered they shared common values and ideas, and Melina was attracted to Tom's kindness and sensitivity. They also liked music and all the same activities.

On the first anniversary of their first date, Tom proposed to Melina. He asked her to stand in a corner with her back to him because he had a surprise. Then he turned her around and proposed. She was so shocked that Tom had to ask her twice before she could answer.

I first met Melina and Tom in May 1996. Melina's parents came along for the planning consultation. It really helps if all the decision makers can be involved in the first planning consultation—discussing budget, visions, etc. A coordinator can suggest ways to achieve the total look the couple wants. I recommend at least three vendors in each category so the couple has a choice, and I never accept a referral fee from my vendors—I refer them based on their past performance.

Melina is a first-grade teacher who lived in Walnut Creek, California, and Tom worked and lived in another city. In addition to her teaching position, Melina was also working on her master's degree. You can imagine how busy she was! At the same time, Melina's parents were planning their son's wedding in September, so things were getting a bit overwhelming. They decided to hire a consultant to keep Mom and other family members from becoming too stressed. By the end of August they also decided to hire me to help with their son's wedding.

THE CEREMONY AND RECEPTION

Both families lived in Sacramento, so Tom and Melina chose the Cathedral of the Blessed Sacrament there for the ceremony site. Tom's uncle, Father Phil, would perform the ceremony. It was my job to find out in advance what other events were being held that day at the ceremony and reception sites, then plan accordingly. As the people were leaving the 5:00 P.M. mass, I was bringing the florist, musicians, etc., in the back door to set up. We also delayed seating the guests until the flowers were placed.

For ceremony music, Tom and Melina chose to have the cathedral organist, as well as the Camellia String Quartet. Melina's aunt, a professional singer, provided the vocals.

They chose Bud Harmon Photography because Bud and his wife, Bonnie, had worked with the family before. In addition to doing beautiful work, Bud and Bonnie have a good understanding of time and worked quickly. I truly feel that the wedding day should not be turned into a "photo shoot." The photographer should understand that this is a time of celebration for family and friends. Because the cathedral was so busy that day, we planned all preceremony photos to be taken in the Capitol Park (or, in case of rain, at the reception site—always have a backup plan).

The Sacramento Grand Ballroom was the reception site. This is a wonderful old bank building that has been converted into a banquet facility—lots of charm. It is only about six blocks from the cathedral, so it was possible to have a carriage drawn by a beautiful white horse to transport the couple from the church to the reception. Whenever possible, it is good to have the ceremony and reception sites fairly close to each other. This is not only easier for the wedding party, but also for the guests.

WEDDING ATTIRE

Melina purchased a Jasmine Italian satin gown decorated with graceful lace calla lilies. Her custom-designed headpiece was highlighted by satin calla lilies cascading down the back. Since Melina is a redhead and stark white didn't complement her skin, she chose candlelight, a soft, creamy white.

Her attendants wore deep plum, floor-length gowns. Extra fabric was purchased for her junior bridesmaid's gown. They also purchased the same fabric as Melina's gown for the flower girl, who was dressed in a lovely white gown that matched the bride's.

Tom selected a black spencer jacket with a mandarin-collar shirt and matching accessories. His groomsmen wore the same tuxedo with plum accessories to match the bridesmaids' gowns. The ring bearer's tuxedo was the same as the groom's. Melina's grandmother made an elegant ring pillow from the same fabric as Melina's dress. The gowns, tuxedos and fabric were all purchased at the same bridal salon. This definitely saves time and money. I only recommend salons that are known for excellent customer service.

FLOWERS AND DECORATIONS

Melina's gown actually set the theme for the flowers. A theme makes it much easier to tie every part of the day together for a good "finished" look. Melina and her attendants carried arm bouquets of calla lilies, guelder roses and freesia. Melina's bouquet was tied with a creamy satin ribbon. The men's boutonnieres were small orchids. The invitations were on creamy white paper decorated with embossed calla lilies, to continue the theme.

Pew bows were made of tulle and flowers, and satin ribbon swagged the family pews. For the reception, the florist designed centerpieces consisting of 36-inch-tall clear glass vases, each containing three tall calla lilies, bear grass and greenery. A beautiful floral swag framed the original old revolving door of the building. The swag was at no cost to the bride because the ballroom had scheduled an advertising photo shoot that day and provided the extra decoration—another reason to find out what else is going on at the site the day of the wedding.

RECEPTION

Melina and Tom opted for a buffet because they wanted their guests to mix and mingle. There was also a hosted bar that served beer and wine. Parking was reserved in a nearby public parking lot and was paid for in advance for the guests' convenience. The guests should not have to pay any cost for coming to the event. Serve only the alcohol you can afford and that you want served. You are not obligated to have a full hosted bar. Try to select a site that has free parking or where you can pay in advance.

The wedding cake was a four-tiered creation decorated with a beautiful fondant bow. It looked like a giant gift. Be sure that the tiers will be supported by dowels. I think I have heard more horror stories about cakes falling over than anything else.

Melina's wedding rings are a family heirloom once worn by Tom's grandmother, and the silver toasting goblets were heirlooms from Melina's grandparents' wedding. Instead of a guest book, they had a 16″ × 20″ photo with a 4″ mat for the guests to sign.

A DJ who also sings was used for the reception music and as an emcee. Tom is a true romantic, and he surprised Melina with a special song for their first dance, "Keeper of the Stars," which was the first song they ever danced to.

They decided not to hire a professional videographer. Friends and family members brought their videocams instead. However, during the reception, the toast was almost missed because the friend who was supposed to tape it had a dead battery. Fortunately, another guest taped it. For reasons like this, professional services should be used whenever possible. The couple cannot recreate the day, and if the photographer or videographer misses a shot, it is lost.

On the wedding day, I keep track of everything—where the bride is, where the groom is, where the rest of the wedding party are wandering off to, what the photographer is doing, whether or not the florist is placing the flowers where we want them, where the musicians are sitting and if they can see my cue, if all the corsages and boutonnieres are pinned on, whether everyone is lined up and inspected before the processional, etc., etc., etc. The bride and her mother certainly shouldn't have to worry over these details!

The total cost of this wedding was under $25,000. ♡

Mimi Doke, Master Bridal Consultant
The Wedding Specialist, Lake Havasu City, Arizona

As a bridal consultant, Mimi works very much like a travel agent in that she receives commissions from the wedding and reception vendors. She feels that because she is most familiar with the local vendors and their prices, she can refer or book the services best suited to the bride. So rather than adding extra expense to the wedding budget, her services as a professional consultant actually save the bride money.

Mimi has contributed a lovely story about a wedding she planned for a firefighter and an elementary school teacher who were living in Rancho Cucamonga, California, but wanted to be married in Lake Havasu City. The couple's dream was to have a wedding on the river with a beach theme, and with Mimi's help that is exactly what they had! ♡

CASE HISTORY # 7

John and Yvonne Dowell

Here's another one of those wonderful blind date stories. A good friend who worked with Yvonne at her elementary school said that her husband worked with a guy at the fire station and asked if Yvonne would like to meet him on a blind date. She said, "Sure," so the four of them went to the Improv, a comedy club. John and Yvonne really hit it off and had a fun evening together.

I asked Yvonne what, after all those years of being single (they were both twenty-eight at the time), made this blind date so special? She said, "We had so much in common, and we got along so well—something clicked."

When John took Yvonne home that night, he told her, "I won't be able to call you for two weeks because I'm studying to take my captain's exam."

She thought to herself, "Oh, sure—I won't hold my breath." But he did call her, and they started dating steadily. John had a boat and they both loved to water-ski, so they spent hours out on the lake enjoying the water.

They met in November 1994, and on Valentine's Day 1996 John proposed to her at a romantic restaurant in Topanga Canyon, California, as they sat outdoors in the moonlight beside a babbling brook with candlelight flickering all around them. Yvonne was totally surprised—and totally ecstatic!

CHOOSING A BRIDAL CONSULTANT

Because John and Yvonne had spent a lot of fun times waterskiing at Lake Havasu, along with a lot of his firemen friends who also loved to hang out there, that's where they wanted to get married. They lived about four hours away, however, which is why they needed the services of a professional bridal consultant to help them with their plans. The day they drove into town and met with Mimi and her assistant, Kari Faulkner, John and Yvonne felt extremely comfortable that they would do an excellent job.

John and Yvonne wanted to accomplish as much as possible during this visit, because once they were back home everything else would need to be planned by phone. During their first visit to meet with Mimi and Kari in Lake Havasu City, they ordered their wedding cake and invitations, chose their ceremony and reception sites and met with the manager of the Bridgeview Room at Shugrue's Garden Gazebo, where they decided on a Hawaiian luau theme. Their buffet-style Polynesian fare included Hawaiian breads, salads, tropical fruits, Hawaiian egg rolls, chicken, beef, shrimp and several pasta dishes.

Shugrue's Bridgeview Room has glass walls that overlook the world-famous London Bridge, and about fifty feet away from Shugrue's is a romantic gazebo near the water, which is where John and Yvonne decided to be married. Yvonne was especially taken with the path that winds from the restaurant to the gazebo, through gardens, over a bridge and around palm trees and fountains. This charming walkway was used for the ceremony processional. Very nice!

WEDDING ATTIRE

Yvonne's wedding dress was an elegant, sophisticated, form-fitting gown, topped with a very simple veil that hung down her back. She carried an equally sophisticated arm bouquet of three long-stemmed calla lilies, tied simply with a white tulle bow.

Her attendants wore coral street-length, fitted dresses with deep

"V" backs, and all the men in the wedding party wore tuxedos.

Because the guests had been asked to wear shorts and Hawaiian shirts to the wedding, which they did, everyone in the wedding party changed into similar attire during the reception. Yvonne wore a Hawaiian flowered sarong and John a shirt of the same fabric with a pair of shorts.

Yvonne's close personal friend, who attended the wedding, styled her hair, as well as the three bridal attendants', and she did a wonderful job.

DECORATIONS

Kari Faulkner took care of all these selections and made the decorations herself. She also designed the cake, the bridal bouquet, Yvonne's attendants' flowers and all the incidentals needed to carry out the Hawaiian theme. The ceremony setting already lent itself to the theme, with its palm trees and waterfalls, so Kari concentrated on decorating the inside of the Bridgeview Room.

She scattered clam shells and Hawaiian confetti of tiny, brightly colored fish and palm trees on the tables, and she created centerpieces out of large fish bowls filled with live goldfish and surrounded by ferns. Each water glass was decorated with a frond that skewered a chunk of pineapple.

The dance floor was framed with huge sand buckets filled with beach shovels, pails and helium balloons, and straw hats were scattered around the room as well, although as the party got going, they were soon donned by the guests. Talented Kari also created two "kissing" gold fish out of balloons that hung above the dance floor. To top off the luau theme, each of the one hundred guests was given a Hawaiian lei to wear during the ceremony and reception.

I must admit this is the first time I've heard of anything like this—at least, during a wedding reception. The firemen decided to swallow all of the centerpieces, which were the live goldfish swimming in fish bowls! Yvonne told me that as soon as they had finished off the goldfish at their own tables, they went around the room trying to buy goldfish from the rest of the guests. The guests got into the spirit of the bidding, trying to raise money for Yvonne's money bag.

After Yvonne described this incredible scene to me, as well as the firemen's enthusiasm for this fish-swallowing competition, I teasingly asked, "Why?" She replied, "Well, you know, they're just a crazy bunch of guys!"

CHOOSING VENDORS

When Mimi heard that the groom was a fireman, she immediately set out to secure the services of Tony Rivello of Sound Waves DJ Service, who also happens to be a fireman. She knew that he would be the best choice because he would be able to interact well with all the firemen attending the wedding. Everyone thought he did a great job!

The photography was done by Mimi Doke, but John and Yvonne chose not to hire a videographer. They were paying for the wedding themselves, and this was one way to save money. They did distribute fifteen disposable cameras, however, which resulted in some fantastic candids, including the firemen taking photos of each other swallowing the goldfish!

The wedding cake consisted of four stair-stepped layers of marbleized chocolate and vanilla that were frosted and topped with colorful fresh flowers. Each layer sat on its own pedestal.

In addition to working closely with the vendors and following up on their responsibilities, Mimi kept a close accounting of the wedding expenses, paying the vendors only after receiving John and Yvonne's approval for each. By doing this, she was able to help John and Yvonne stay well within their wedding budget of $15,000.

To prevent any last minute problems, Mimi double-checked with all the vendors the day before the wedding, confirming their duties and delivery times. She also maintained a master file that contained samples and color swatches of everything for the wedding and reception, including the cake, flowers, decorations, and so forth. This file helped ensure that everything would be color-coordinated.

On the wedding day itself, because Mimi was occupied with the photography, Kari Faulkner served as Yvonne's personal wedding day coordinator, which Yvonne said, "gave me great peace of mind."

Lodging was also arranged for the wedding party and most of the guests, who stayed at the London Bridge Resort in Lake Havasu City.

John and Yvonne said that Mimi and Kari did a "fantastic job, and we definitely could not have done it without them. The comments we heard from our guests were that it was the 'funnest wedding' with the best food and most beautiful decorations."

John and Yvonne's wedding weekend was just exactly what they had hoped it would be: a relaxed, fun time for everyone, with plenty of waterskiing. It was so stress-free, in fact, that John and Yvonne were able to spend the morning of their wedding skiing on Lake Havasu.

Can't get much more worry-free than that! ♡

After reading all these wonderful stories and considering the benefits of hiring a professional to coordinate your wedding, you may decide to locate a member of the Association of Bridal Consultants who lives near you. You can do this very easily by calling the association number listed in the appendix. If you would like to contact one of the Master Bridal Consultants featured in this chapter, their addresses and telephone numbers are listed there as well.

My thanks go to all these consultants for sharing their helpful inside wedding-planning tips, and I also thank the couples themselves who so graciously shared their stories.

THINGS TO REMEMBER:

○ You should have some agreement with your consultant in writing. A formal contract probably is not necessary; a letter of agreement, signed by both of you, is usually enough.

○ If you want to plan part of your wedding yourself, don't worry that a consultant will want to run the whole show. A professional bridal consultant will work with you, handling as much or as little of your wedding as you want. After all, it is your wedding. The consultant is there to help make your day perfect.

○ It is normal for a consultant to charge about 15 percent of the cost of the wedding. Some consultants charge an hourly rate or a fixed fee, or some a combination of these. Others charge nothing and earn their income from supplier commissions. All these methods are acceptable, but you should determine in advance how your consultant will be paid.

○ Using a bridal consultant need not be expensive. In fact, you can often save money because a consultant can suggest less expensive alternatives that still enhance your wedding. Consultants are often able to obtain discounts from suppliers.

○ Members of the Association of Bridal Consultants pledge to:
  • Represent each client fairly and honestly, providing all agreed-to services in a timely and cost-efficient manner
  • Establish reasonable and proper fees for services and provide written estimates to each client
  • Use honest, factual advertising
  • Operate an establishment that is a credit to the community

I hope that one of my worry-free wedding ideas is exactly what you had hoped to find within the pages of this book. I'm sure you found many of them to be revelations, because as I did my research, they were a bonanza to me, and I thought I'd heard it all!

You may decide on a Venue Wedding where the site coordinator plans everything for you or a Destination Wedding where you can be married in a worry-free ceremony at your honeymoon site.

Of course, one of the casual weddings may be for you—especially if this is a second marriage and the emphasis this time is on "fun."

Finally, if you have your heart set on a formal wedding with all the trimmings, you can still avoid the hassles by following my do-it-yourself worry-free hints or by letting a professional handle everything.

Whatever type of wedding you choose, however, here is one last word of advice: Keep your sense of humor.

Nothing beats a sense of humor for relieving stress in any situation, but especially when planning a wedding. So, lighten up and don't take it all so seriously. Everything will work out—you'll see! And when it does, let me know about it. I'd love to hear from you.

Write me in care of my publisher at:
Betterway Books • 1507 Dana Avenue • Cincinnati, Ohio 45207

Good luck and have a wonderful wedding!

2

CHAPTER I - THE VENUE WEDDING

American Bed & Breakfast Association, P.O. Box 1387, Midlothian, VA 23113; (804) 379-2222.

American Bed & Breakfast Association's Inspected, Rated and Approved: Bed & Breakfasts and Country Inns, 5th ed. Edited by Beth Stuhlman; published in April 1996 by American Bed & Breakfast Association. $17.95.

America's Best Bed & Breakfasts, 2nd ed. By Fodor's Travel Staff; published in April 1997 by Fodor's Travel Publications. $18.00.

Belhurst Castle, Route 14 South, P. O. Box 609, Geneva, NY 14456; (315) 781-0201.

Captain Walsh House, 235 East L Street, Benicia, CA 94510; (707) 747-5653.

The Complete Guide to Bed & Breakfasts, Inns and Guesthouses: In the United States, Canada and Worldwide, 14th ed. By Pamela Lanier; published in December, 1996 by Ten Speed Press. $16.95.

East Fork Country Estate, 9875 S.E. 222nd, Gresham, OR 97080; (503) 667-7069.

Four Seasons Hotel, 120 East Delaware Place, Chicago, IL 60611; (312) 280-8800; fax: (312) 280-9184.

Holiday Inn, 7800 S. Kingery Highway, Willowbrook, IL 60521; (630) 325-6400.

Hyatt Regency Monterey, One Old Golf Course Road, Monterey, CA 93940; (408) 372-1234.

Hyatt Worldwide Reservations, (800) 233-1234.
Note: The operators who answer this number may not know about wedding or honey-

moon packages at a specific Hyatt Regency, but they can furnish you with the direct telephone number of each resort location where you should ask to speak to their "Special Events Coordinator" or "Wedding Specialist," who will provide you with detailed information for that site.

Quail Lodge Resort and Golf Club, 8000 Valley Greens Drive, Carmel, CA 93923; (408) 624-1581 (the wedding coordinator is at ext. 360).

The Queen Mary, Queen Mary Seaport, 1126 Queens Highway, Long Beach, CA 90802-6390; (562) 435-3511. *The Hotel Queen Mary* 562-499-1688

The Sagamore, Bolton Landing, NY 12814-0450; (518) 644-9400.

Sara's Bed and Breakfast Inn, 941 Heights Blvd., Houston, TX 77008; (713) 868-1130 or (800) 593-1130.

Troutbeck, Leedsville Road, Amenia, NY 12501; (914) 373-9681; website: http://www.troutbeck.com

Weddings in Sedona, Sandy Ezrine, P.O. Box 10627, Sedona, AZ 86339; (800) 973-3762; fax: (520) 639-4535; e-mail: romance@sedona.net; website: http://www.wedguide.com/sedona.html

CHAPTER 2 - DESTINATION WEDDINGS INSIDE MAINLAND U.S.

Association of Bridal Consultants, 200 Chestnutland Road, New Milford, CT 06776-2521; (860) 355-0464; fax: (860) 354-1404; e-mail: bridalassn@aol.com Note: Call the Association to locate a member in your honeymoon city, or you may want to call one of these members who specializes in planning destination weddings at various honeymoon locations inside mainland U.S.

Arkansas

Margie Bullock, Best Western Eureka Inn, Hwy 62 and 23N, Eureka Springs, AR 72632; (501) 253-9551.

That Special Touch, Jo Swofford, RR 2, Box 292, Berryville, AR 72616; (870) 423-2861.

Connecticut

Steve Ledewitz, Worldtek Travel, 111 Water Street, New Haven, CT 06511; (203) 772-0470.

Disneyland, Anaheim, California

Disneyland Resort, Lisa Simpson, 1150 W. Cerritos Ave., Anaheim, CA 92802; (714) 956-6715.

Florida

A Bride's Dream, Anne Lentz, 9344 Toby Lane, Orlando, FL 32817; (407) 678-0933.

Delicious Treasures, Tabitha Wilson, 1126 S. Goldwyn Ave., Orlando, FL 32805; (407) 293-9510.

Just Marry! Susan Southerland, 845 Sand Lake Road, Orlando, FL 32809; (407) 876-5500.

Keepsake Floral, Inc., Dana Adkinson, 724 Brookhaven Drive, Orlando, FL 32814; (800) 616-KEEP.

Idaho

Tammy Schneider, Coeur d'Alene Resort, P.O. Box 7200, Coeur d'Alene, ID 83816; (800) 365-8338.

Las Vegas

Best Bet Wedding Consultant, Carolyn Hall, 4001 S. Decatur Blvd., #37470, Las Vegas, NV 89103; (702) 257-7768.

Cherished Moments, Lisa Wainscott, 8137 Exploration Ave., Las Vegas, NV 89131; (702) 395-4217.

Crafty Creations, Donajean Anderson, 4225 Fidus Drive, #210, Las Vegas, NV 89103; (702) 248-6061.

Moments to Cherish, Zipporah Singleton, 5000 E. Bonanza Rd., #386, Las Vegas, NV 89110; (702) 452-5160.

The Mountains of Colorado

Jenny Gloudemans, P.O. Box 38, Keystone, CO 80435; (970) 468-4307.

Rocky Mountain Celebrations, Kelly Abramson or Angela Carlevato, P.O. Box 2680, Breckenridge, CO 80424; (970) 468-8403.

The Wedding Planner, Inc., Bernie Briggs, P.O. Box 1814, Vail, CO 81658; (970) 949-9464.

Wendee Walter, Holiday Inn, P.O. Box 4310, Frisco, CO 80443; (800) 782-7669.

South Carolina

A Creative Charleston Wedding, Margie Carley, P.O. Box 60481, Charleston, SC 29419; (800) 354-9303.

Leesa Padgett, Ashley Florist, 29 Magnolia Road, Charleston, SC 29407; (803) 556-3070.

Southern Weddings With Style, Lisa Parker, P.O. Box 23644, Hilton Head Island, SC 29925; (803) 689-9333.

Weddings & Events, Cheryl Cox, P.O. Box 7121, Myrtle Beach, SC 29577; (803) 449-0597.

A Wonderful Wedding, Linda Thomason, 2011B Bee's Ferry Road, Charleston, SC 39414; (803) 556-1500.

Tennessee

Crowne Plaza, Jean Cannon, 623 Union St., Nashville, TN 37219; (615) 742-6043.

Opryland Hotel, Robin Schappert, 2800 Opryland Drive, Nashville, TN 37214; (615) 871-6855.

Vermont

Stratton Mountain Inn, David VonAchen, Middle Ridge Road, Stratton Mountain, VT 05155; (802) 297-2500.

The Wedding Wizard, Riki Bowen, P.O. Box 9307, South Burlington, VT 05407; (802) 862-5557.

Venues featured in Chapter 2

Caesars Pocono Resorts, (800) 233-4141 (for their "drive-in" packages) or (800) 432-9932 (for their "air-inclusive" packages) or (800) 257-3201 (to contact one of their wedding consultants); website: http://www.caesars.com

Cal-Neva Resort, P.O. Box 368, Crystal Bay, NV 89402; (800) CAL-NEVA or (702) 832-4000; fax: (702) 832-0505; e-mail: calneva@sierra.net

Disney's Fairy Tale Weddings, P.O. Box 10,000, Lake Buena Vista, FL 32830-1000; (407) 828-3400; fax: (407) 828-3744.

Mountain Valley Chapel, P.O. Box 1550; Pigeon Forge, TN 37868; (800) 729-4365; e-mail: glucas@esper.com; website: http://www.mvchapel.com

Teton Mountain Weddings, P.O. Box 30046, Jackson Hole, WY 83001; (800) 842-0391, (307) 739-0395; fax: (307) 734-1655; e-mail: kbrody@ wyoming.com; website: http://www.jimedia.com/tetonweddings/

Treasure Island, P.O. Box 7711, Las Vegas, NV 89193-7711; (702) 894-7111.

Wedding Chapel at Caesars, P.O. Box 6930, Stateline, NV 89449; (800) 833-4422.

CHAPTER 3 - DESTINATION WEDDINGS OUTSIDE MAINLAND U.S.

Note: When dialing a foreign country—except for Canada and those countries in the Caribbean that have an 809 area code—you must always dial "011" before dialing the number. This is called the International Dialing Indicator and indicates to your long distance carrier that you are dialing a number outside the U.S.

Association of Bridal Consultants, 200 Chestnutland Road, New Milford, CT 06776-2521; (860) 355-0464; fax: (860) 354-1404; e-mail: bridalassn@aol.com
Note: Call the association to locate a member in your honeymoon city or call one of these members who specialize in planning destination weddings outside mainland U.S.

The Caribbean

Lee-Ann Bean, 13 South Court Ave., Paget, Bermuda PG06; (441) 236-7948.

Iraida Davila, 249 FD Roosevelt Ave., Hato Rey, Puerto Rico 00918; (809) 750-4786.

Fantasia Occasions, Debra Williams, 168 Crown Bay #310, St. Thomas, Virgin Islands 00802; (800) 326-8272.

Shelly Hamill, P.O. Box 228, Crawl Hill Post Office, Hamilton Parish, Bermuda CRBX; (441) 293-4033.

Macie Hanna, P.O. Box N-1843, Nassau, Bahamas; (242) 323-2709.

Minerva Lugo, Jose Fidalgo Diaz 1977, Caldas, RP, Puerto Rico 00926; (787) 760-6743.

Margarita Ruiz-Montilla, Belen #11 De San Patricio, Guaynabo, Puerto Rico 00968; (787) 792-4571.

Weddings in the Bahamas, Anne Williams, P.O. Box N10155, Nassau, Bahamas; (242) 322-2677.

Cruise-Related Weddings

Sue Bulmer, Cruise Holidays, 11032 Montgomery NE, Albuquerque, NM 87111; (505) 296-6255.

A Wedding for You, Karen Emery, Owner, 10860 Southwest 38th Drive, Davie, FL 33328-1328; (954) 472-0320, (800) 929-4198; fax: (954) 473-9932; e-mail: tieknot1@aol.com; website: http://www.aweddingforyou.com

Germany

Wonderful Weddings and Parties, Fredericka Johns, Sollner Str. 50, 81479 Munchen, Germany; 49-89-791-1985.

Hawaii

Aston Wailea Resort, Laura de la Nux, 3700 Wailea Alanui, Wailea, Maui, HI 96753; (808) 879-1922.

Beaches-N-Dreams, Vicki Tuttle, 73-4764 Halolani St., Kailua Kona, HI 96740; (808) 325-5213.

A Dream Wedding: Maui Style, Tracy Flanagan, 143 Dickenson Street, Lahaina, HI 96761; (808) 661-1777.

Marry Me Maui, Vanessa Hartley, 63A Olinda Road, Makawao, HI 96768; (800) 745-0344.

A Wedding Made in Hawaii, Alicia Laurel, P.O. Box 986, Kihei, HI 96753; (800) 453-3440.

Weddings By Lise, Lise Padron, P.O. Box 25862, Honolulu, HI 96825; (808) 591-0025.

Mexico
Diseno Nupcial, Luz Millan Vargas, Blvd. Lomas De La Hda #14, Atizapan, Edo.De, Mexico 52925; 52-5-370-8395 (this consultant lives in Mexico City).

Singapore
Just Married Wedding Planners, Michael AuKahWai and Andre Danker, 276 E. Coast Road, The KyoJinKai, Singapore 428943; 65-346-0276.

Weddings Anywhere In The World
Intimate Weddings, Vikki Williams, 1709-1/2 E. 87th St. #152, Chicago, IL 60617; (773) 288-3476.

Venues and vendors mentioned in Chapter 3
American Hawaii Cruises, 2 N. Riverside Plaza, Chicago, IL 60606; Wedding Coordinator: (800) 765-7000, ext. 6014.

Casa Turquesa, Cancun, Mexico, 52-98-85-2924.

Cruise Lines, Inc., 150 N.W. 168th St., North Miami Beach, FL 33169; (800) 777-0707.

Delta's Dream Vacation Center, (800) 872-7786.

Fiesta America Coral Beach, Cancun, Mexico, 52-988-32900.

Four Seasons Resort Maui at Wailea, 3900 Wailea Alanui, Wailea, Maui, HI 96753; (800) 334-6284 or (800) 332-3442.

The Halekulani on Waikiki Beach, 2199 Kalia Road, Honolulu, HI 96815-1988; (800) 367-2343.

Half Moon Golf, Tennis and Beach Club, P.O. Box 80, Montego Bay, Jamaica, West Indies; (809) 953-2211; fax: (809) 953-2731; website: http://www.changes.com/HalfMoon/home.html

Hyatt Regency, Cancun, Mexico, P.O. Box 1201, Cancun, Q.R. 77500 Mexico; 52-988-3-09-66.

Hyatt Regency Kauai Resort & Spa, 1571 Poipu Road, Koloa, Kauai, HI 96756; (800) 233-1234, (808) 742-1234; fax: (808) 742-1557.

La Casa que Canta, Acapulco, Mexico, 91-800-093-45.

Las Brisas, Acapulco, Mexico, 52-74-84-1580.

Namale Resort, Box 244, Savusavu, Fiji; (800) 727-FIJI, or 9191 Towne Centre Drive, Suite 600, San Diego, CA 92122; (619) 535-6380; fax: (619) 535-6385; e-mail: namalefiji@aol.com

Pineapple Beach Club, P.O. Box 54, St. John's, Antigua, West Indies; (809) 463-2006, (407) 994-5640.

Sandals Resorts, represented by Unique Vacations, Inc., 4950 S.W. 72nd Avenue, 2nd floor, Miami, FL 33155; (800) SANDALS, (305) 284-1300; fax: (305) 667-8996; or contact your favorite travel agent who will make your reservations.

SuperClubs Lido Resorts and SuperClubs Breezes Resorts, (800) GO SUPER, (954) 925-0925.

Note: When calling resorts in Mexico, I find it helpful to speak very slowly and clearly when I say, "I want to talk to the person who plans *weddings*." The word "weddings" always seems to get me in touch with the right person. (Whatever you do, don't ask about their "wedding packages" because they will think you want to deliver wedding packages to a guest in the hotel.)

CHAPTER 4

Helpful website if planning an Internet wedding:
  http://www.loop.com/~cyberlove

CHAPTER 5

National Certification Board for Therapeutic Massage, (800) 296-0664.

CHAPTER 6

Master Bridal Consultants featured in this chapter

Nancy DeProspo, Humbug Associates, 335 Pine Ridge Circle, Suite A2, Greenacres, FL 33463; (561) 439-6495; e-mail: nancyd@mail.idt.net

Mimi Doke, The Wedding Specialist, 1425 McCulloch Blvd., Suite F, Lake Havasu City, AZ 86403; (520) 453-6000; fax: (520) 453-3001.

Helen Louie, Mother of the Bride, 5738 Stokely Court, Orangevale, CA 95662; (916) 989-1787, (888) 933-6448, (888) WEDNG4U; e-mail: hlouie@aol.com

Mary Rahal, Waldorf Engraving and Printing, 11504 Timberbrook Dr., Waldorf, MD 20601; (301) 645-0320 or 843-7165.

Cheri Rice, The Personal Touch Bridal Agency, 15210 Waco Street N.W., Anoka, MN 55303; (612) 421-4525.

Jo Ann Swofford, That Special Touch, R.R. #2, Box 292, Berryville, AR 72616-9559; (501) 423-2861; e-mail: pbj-tst@cswnet.com

Sue Winner, Sue Winner and Associates, 333 Sandy Springs Circle, Suite 130, Atlanta, GA 30328; (888) BEMARRIED; fax: (404) 851-9923; e-mail: winwed@mindspring.com

Accredited Bridal Consultants, 113
American Bed & Breakfast Association, 144
American Hawaii Cruises, 45-46, 150
Anniversary party wedding, 79
Antigua, 60-62
Arizona
    "denim-required" wedding, 69
    Lake Havasu City, 136
    Sedona, 8-11
Arkansas
    Berryville, 118-119
    destination weddings in, 145
Aruba, 66
Association of Bridal Consultants, 40, 113, 142,
    145, 148
Attendants
    attire, 100-102
    expenses, 87
Attire, wedding party, 99-102
A Wedding for You, 57, 149

Bahamas, 60, 65. See also Caribbean wedding
Basic Wedding, The (Carnival Cruise), 54
Beach party wedding, 68-69
Beavers, John and Tammy, 114-118
Bed and breakfast wedding, 5-8
Belhurst Castle, 19, 144
Billiards table wedding, 81-82
Bridal consultants case studies,
    113-142
Bridal show, 94
Bride's family, expenses paid by,
    86-87
Brody, Karen, 36-37
Budget, 86-88
Budget Planner form, 87-89

Caesars
    Lake Tahoe, 28, 148
    Pocono Resorts, 30-31, 148
California
    Anaheim, 24, 146
    Benicia, 5-6

Disneyland, 146
    Long Beach, 15-16
    Monterey, 11-12
    Quail Lodge Resort, 14, 145
    Sacramento, 132
    San Francisco, 70
    Yosemite National Park, 70
Cal-Neva Lodge, 25-28, 148
Captain Walsh House, 5-6, 144
Caribbean wedding, 53-66
Carnival Cruise Line wedding packages, 54, 56
Case studies, 113-142
Castle wedding, 19
Caterer, 97-98
Celebrity Cruise Line wedding packages, 55-56
Ceremony site
    hints and questions about, 95-96
    on wedding day, 106
Chao, Susan and Michael, 128-132
Christmas wedding, 79
Cinderella Wedding. See Castle wedding;
    Disney's Fairy Tale Weddings
Classic Car Show wedding, 82
Classic Cruise Ship Wedding (Norwegian Line),
    55
Clothing. See Attire, wedding party
Club function weddings, 76-78
Colorado mountains, 147
Combination wedding. See Surprise wedding
Contracts, 41
Cornwell, Lynn and Andy, 57-60
Country Inn Wedding Weekends (Troutbeck),
    4-5
Country-Western theme, 93. See also Teton
    Mountain Weddings
Cruise Lines, Inc., 53, 56, 150
Cruise-related weddings
    addresses, 149
    American Hawaii Cruises, 45-46, 150
    Caribbean, 53-60

Decorations, 104
Delta's Dream Vacations, 61, 150

Deluxe Romance Wedding (Carnival Cruise), 54
"Denim Required" wedding, 69
DeProspo, Nancy, 127-132, 152
Destination wedding
   inside mainland U.S., 21-41, 145-148
   outside mainland U.S., 42-67, 148-152
Diamond Radiance wedding package (Mountain
   Valley Chapel), 32
Diamond Treasures wedding package (Treasure
   Island), 29
Diamond Wedding package (Majesty Cruise), 55
Dickerson, Lee and Inge, 17-19
Dinner themes, 12
Disney's Fairy Tale Weddings, 23-25, 148
Dogsled wedding, 36-37
Do-It-Yourself Worry-Free Wedding. See
   Worry-Free Wedding
Doke, Mimi, 136-142, 152
Dowell, John and Yvonne, 137-141
Duran, Sulema, 52
Durrett, Christy and Adam, 34-36

East Fork Country Estate, 5, 144
Elegant Paradise wedding package (Princess
   Cruise), 55
Emerald Wedding (Majesty Cruise), 55
Emergency kit, 106
Emery, Karen, 57, 59, 149
Esterquest, Tom and Anne, 48-51
Ezrine, Sandy, 8, 10-11, 69, 145

Family gathering wedding, 78-81
Family Medallion Service (Mountain Valley
   Chapel), 32-33
Family reunion wedding, 78
Favors, 104
Fiji wedding, 46-51
Flight of Love wedding (Sedona), 8
Florida
   destination weddings, 147
   Greenacres, 127
   Orlando, 23
Flowers, 102, 106
Four Seasons Hotel (Chicago), 15-19, 144
Four Seasons Resort (Maui), 43-44, 151

Garden wedding, 4-5, 92
Georgia, Atlanta, 120
Germany, 149

Gold Treasures wedding package (Treasure
   Island), 29
Gray, Tiffany and Michael, 108
Groom's family, expenses paid by, 87
Grusky, Scott, 82-84

Halekulani, The (Waikiki Beach),
   44-45, 151
Half Moon Resort, 62-63, 151
Hawaii
   addresses, 149-151
   Kauai, 42-43, 45-46
   Maui, 43-44
   Oahu, 42-44
Hawaiian theme, 92, 139
Hawaii wedding, 42-46. See also Hawaii; Hawai-
   ian theme
Hockey game wedding, 82
Holiday Inn, 12-13, 144
Holland America wedding packages, 54
Honeymoon packages
   cruise ship, 56-57
   Endless Love (Cal-Neva), 26
   Halekulani, 44
   Pineapple Beach Club, 61-62
   Poconos, 30-31
   Sandals Resorts, 60
Honeymoon Wedding. See Destination
   Wedding
Hotel wedding, 11-15
Houseboat wedding, 71
Humbug Associates, 127-132, 152
Hunt, Lisa and Andy, 83-84
Hyatt Regency Resorts
   Cancun, 51-53, 151
   Kauai Resort, 45, 151
   Monterey, 11-12, 144
   Worldwide Reservations, 144-145

Idaho, destination weddings, 146
Illinois
   Chicago, 15
   Willowbrook, 13
Informal wedding, 68-84
Internet wedding, 82, 152

Jackson, Rhonda and Tim, 37-40
Jamaica, 60-65

Kelly, Mimi and Brian, 9-11
K.I.S.S. wedding, 68-74

Lake Tahoe wedding, 25-28
Las Vegas wedding, 28-30, 146
Limousine service, 104
Lokelani Wedding (Four Seasons Resort), 44
Louie, Helen, 132-136, 152

Majesty Cruise Line wedding packages, 55
Maryland, Waldorf, 114
Massage Therapist, 112, 152
Master Bridal Consultants case studies, 113-142
Mexico
    Acapulco, 53
    Cancun, 51-53
    Mexico City, 53, 150
Millam, Daniel and Sandra, 118-119
Minnesota, Anoka, 124
Montego Bay, 60, 62-64
Mother of the Bride, 132-136, 152
Mothers' attire, 101-102
Mountain Valley Chapel, 32-36, 148
Mountain wedding, 31-40
Musicians, 103

Namale Resort (Fiji), 47-51, 151
Nani Kai Wedding Package (American Hawaii
    Cruises), 45-46
Nassau, 64
Nature wedding, 8-11
Negril, 63
Nevada wedding
    Lake Tahoe, 25-28
    Las Vegas, 28-30
New York
    Armenia, 4
    Bolton Landing, 13-14
    Geneva, 19
    New York City, 4
Norwegian Cruise Line wedding packages, 55
Novelty wedding, 81-82

Ocho Rios, 63
One-Stop Wedding. See Venue Wedding
On-Island Wedding in St. Thomas (Carnival
    Cruise), 54
On-the-water wedding, 15-19
Oregon, Gresham, 5

Participation wedding, 69-70
Party wedding, 75
Patio party wedding, 70
Pearl Treasures wedding package (Treasure
    Island), 29
Pearl Wedding package (Majesty Cruise), 55
Pennsylvania, Poconos, 30-31
Personal Touch Bridal Agency, The, 124-127,
    152
Petite Cruise Ship Wedding (Norwegian Cruise),
    55
Photographer, 103-104, 107
Picnic wedding
    Fourth of July, 79
    in the park, 70
Pigeon Forge wedding, 32-36
Pineapple Beach Club, 61-62, 151
Platinum Treasures wedding package (Treasure
    Island), 29
Plumeria Wedding (Four Seasons Resort), 44
Poconos wedding, 30-31
Polynesian theme, 70
    Holiday Inn, 13
    See also Hawaiian theme
Princess Cruises wedding packages, 54-55
Professional Bridal Consultants, 113

Quail Lodge Resort and Golf Club, 14, 145
Queen Anne Wedding Package (Sara's Bed and
    Breakfast Inn), 7
Queen Mary ocean liner, 15-18, 145

Rahal, Mary, 114-118, 152
Rakich, Karen and Steve, 26-28
Reception food and drink, 97-98
Reception site
    hints and questions about, 96-97
    on wedding day, 106-107
Renaissance Wedding. See Castle wedding
Resort wedding, 11-15
Rice, Cheri, 124-127, 152
Robbins, Tony, 47, 49-50
Romantic candlelight theme, 93
Royal Caribbean wedding packages, 56
Ruby Wedding package (Majesty Cruise), 55
Ruskin, Myrna, 1

Sagamore, The, 13-14, 145
St. Lucia, 60

St. Thomas, 53-57
Sandals Resorts, 60-61, 151
Sapphire Wedding package (Majesty Cruise), 55
Sara's Bed and Breakfast Inn, 7-8, 145
Shipboard wedding. *See* On-the-water wedding
Shoreside Wedding in St. Thomas (Carnival
    Cruise), 54
Silver Treasures wedding package (Treasure
    Island), 29
Singapore, 150
Ski lift wedding, 82
Skydiving wedding, 82
South Carolina, 147
Space Needle wedding, 81
Special Value Package (Royal Caribbean), 56
Sports get-together weddings, 75-76
Stress, 1, 143
SuperClubs
    addresses, 151
    Breezes, 64
    Lido Resorts, 63
Surprise wedding, 74-81
    club functions, 76-78
    family gatherings, 78-81
    parties, 75
    sports get-togethers, 75-76
Swofford, Jo Ann, 118-120, 145, 152

Taitz, Nona and Kevin, 121-124
Tennessee
    destination weddings, 147
    Pigeon Forge, 31-36
Teton Mountain Weddings, 36-40, 148
Thanksgiving Day wedding, 79-81
That Special Touch, 118-120, 145, 152
Theme park wedding, 70
Themes
    worry-free, 92-93
    See also specific wedding themes
Thompson, Shari and Keith, 80-81
To-do list, 88, 90-92
Transportation, 104
Travel Wedding. *See* Destination Wedding
Treasure Island wedding packages, 28-30, 148
Tropical weddings. *See* Caribbean wedding; Fiji

wedding; Hawaii; Hawaiian theme; Hawaii
    wedding; Polynesian theme
Tropical Paradise package (Princess Cruise), 54
Troutbeck, 4-5, 145

Ultimate Paradise package (Princess Cruise), 55

Venue wedding, 3-20, 144
    advantages and disadvantages, 3-4
    bed and breakfast, 5-8
    castle wedding, 19
    garden wedding, 4
    hotel wedding, 11-15
    nature wedding, 8-11
    on-the-water wedding, 15-19
    resort wedding, 11-15
Vermont, 147-148
Victorian Wedding. *See* Castle wedding
Videographer, 103-104, 107
Virgin Islands
    British, 66
    U.S., 65-66
    See also St. Thomas

Waldorf Engraving and Printing, 114-118, 152
Washington, Seattle, 81
Wedding announcements, 41
Wedding cake, 98-99
Wedding gown, 99-100
WeddingMoon package (Sandals), 61
Weddings of a Lifetime, 23, 82
Wedding Specialist, The, 136-142, 152
Weddings in Sedona, 8-11, 69, 145
Welcome Aboard Wedding package (Carnival
    Cruise), 54
Wiltjer, Peter and Kylie, 124-127
Winner, Sue, 120-124, 152
Worry-Free Wedding, 85-112
    budget, 86-88
    hints and questions to ask, 95-105
    suppliers, 93-95
    themes, 92-93
    to-do list, 88, 90-92
    wedding day, 105-107
Wyoming, Jackson Hole, 36, 148